CLARENCE HOLBROOK CARTER

Clarence Holbrook Carter in backroom of studio with *Icon Concentric Space*. Photographed in 1982 by Michael Bergman

CLARENCE HOLBROOK CARTER

TEXT BY
FRANK ANDERSON TRAPP
DOUGLAS DREISHPOON
RICARDO PAU-LLOSA

FOREWORD BY
JAMES A. MICHENER

RIZZOLI
NEW YORK

A Chameleon Book

First published in the United States of America in 1989 by
RIZZOLI INTERNATIONAL PUBLICATIONS, INC.
597 Fifth Avenue
New York, NY 10017

Produced by Chameleon Books, Inc.
31 Smith Road, Chesterfield, Massachusetts 01012

Production director/designer: Arnold Skolnick
Editorial director: Marion Wheeler
Associate editors: David Frankel, Stephen Frankel, Vicki Brooks
Editorial assistant: Ellen Dibble
Design assistant : Nancy Crompton
Composition: Ultracomp, New York
Production services: Four Colour Imports, Ltd., Louisville, Kentucky
Printed and bound by Everbest Printing Company, Ltd., Hong Kong

Library of Congress Cataloging-in-Publication Data

Trapp, Frank.
    Clarence Holbrook Carter.

    Bibliography: p.
    Includes index.
    1. Carter, Clarence Holbrook, 1904 –   — Criticism
and interpretation. I. Dreishpoon, Douglas.
II. Pau-Llosa, Ricardo. III. Title.
ND237.C287T73 1989   759.13   88-42701
ISBN 0-8478-0975-7

ACKNOWLEDGMENTS

Chameleon Books thanks the ACA Galleries, Gimpel & Weitzenhoffer Ltd., and Hirschl & Adler Galleries for their assistance in the preparation of this book. Grateful acknowledgment is made to the following for their excellent photographic services: Michael Bergman, Mary Beth Campbell, Marcia Goldner, Roy Green, Fred Jacobs, and Ann Oakes. We wish to extend our gratitude to Clarence Holbrook Carter for his cooperation. And finally, we thank Vicki Brooks and Charles Varga for suggesting that Clarence Holbrook Carter is an artist whose time for greater recognition has come.

CONTENTS

Foreword by James A. Michener

For some time I have suspected that forty years from now American collectors and museums will be searching for examples of Clarence Carter's work. His canvases will be appreciated both as masterful demonstrations of the painterly art and as high points of abstract surrealism.

There will always be a widespread interest in surrealism as one manner of reacting to physical phenomena. Granted, it will not constitute the major concern of art, but it will enjoy a permanent niche, if only because of the scintillating sidelight it throws upon human experience. Carter's work, which constitutes some of the best surrealist painting done in America, compares favorably with the imaginary visions of Max Ernest, Matta, and Kay Sage. In the field of abstract surrealism, I believe that Carter stands pretty much at the head of the class. His vision is exceptionally pure, his technique is unsurpassed; such a union produces works of great visual impact and tactile delight.

He works in three styles, and his admirers seem about equally divided in their preferences. *Over and Aboves,* for which he has been most noted, are tall canvases divided horizontally near the middle. The lower portion consists of a blank wall, resembling the side of an adobe house. Leering out from a background above the wall is some huge animal or bird, its chin often resting on top of the wall (one is a water buffalo, another a vulture). Some viewers find them particularly menacing, while others see them as evocative of the spirit of the animal kingdom. Effective they are: one man's view of nature as perceived in a vision. They avoid the purely fanciful constructions of wildlife as seen in certain surrealist paintings, and because of this, they might be criticized for showing a lack of imagination. Yet they are so forceful in their imagery that they command the viewer's attention. They are very successful in conveying a sense of the mystery of animal life, and ought to be of increasing interest as we begin to grapple with the ecological problem of what man's relationship to nature should be. In this respect they fulfill admirably one of the demands of surrealist art: by jolting our senses with a bright new vision of ordinary things, it prompts us to reconsider these things with new intellectual concepts. In this series, it is the surrealist half of abstract surrealism that dominates.

A *Mandala* consists of a series of superimposed, translucent egg-shapes floating in space and interlocking in both design and color. They are beautifully intricate and each comes to focus in a series of increasingly smaller shapes which end in a minute, brilliantly colored central image—out of which all the other forms seem to have expanded. Color is sovereign. First there is the huge expanse of background, usually in a subdued flat color; then the evanescent ovoid shapes in a complementary color; then the minute central core in a brilliant and contrasting hue; and finally, across the bottom, a broad band of an entirely new and vibrating color which seems to have been arbitrarily selected for its shock value. *The result is a marvelous blend of harmonious movement, forward and backward oscillation of the forms, and vibrations of colors. There is something quite mysterious about these constructions. Although they represent the interaction of pure form and color, they do so in a way that captivates the imagination. In the dualism represented by the term "abstract surrealism," these works stress the former. Their high imaginative content makes them more than mere abstractions, since they are infused with the mysteriousness that is essential to any good surrealist representation.

Transections represent the apex of Carter's art. In unworldly landscapes, innumerable cells disappear into the far distance or move upward and outward into space without definition. In this way a non-finite universe is established. In each cell, or emerging from it, appears an egg-shaped form, point down; these seem to be in upward motion, with a strong sense of having just been born. Because the visual imagery is so much more powerful than in the *Mandalas,* the colors can be more subdued. The total effect is quite powerful —an almost ideal blending of the abstract and the surreal.

To me, *Transection #3: After Fra Angelico* is one of the best paintings Carter has done. I saw it before it was titled and supposed that the coffin in the foreground had been taken from an early Renaissance painter such as Orcagna or Castagno. Then I remembered something Carter had once written—"I have always considered Giovanni di Paolo a great abstract surrealist painter"—and concluded that he had borrowed his central theme from this delightful Sienese. So I thought to myself, What a felicitous borrowing. It fits the requirements perfectly. Only later did I discover that the coffin had come from a work by Fra Angelico.

If ever a painting superbly illustrated the essence of the Resurrection, it is this—with the empty coffin in the foreground, the endless crypts reaching into the distance, the marvelous scattering of graveyard slabs. The assembly of images alone would make this a notable surrealist painting, but when the ascending ovoid shape is considered, the essential element of the Resurrection become one of Carter's most memorable paintings, for it has that timeless quality which marks all great surrealist works.

More universal and less explicit, I believe, is *Transection #8,* 1970. The cell-like structures are very abstract, the horizon is infinite, the colors have no literary significance, and the emerging ovoid forms have a mysteriousness not evident in the preceding work. This is a tremendously satisfying painting, and the various elements coalesce in a remarkable way. The simplicity of design and execution makes it especially attractive, and it is perhaps one of Carter's most balanced achievements in terms of striving for an abstract/surrealist symbiosis.

The excellence of Carter's work will be increasingly appreciated, I think as its consistently high quality is recognized. His paintings grow in depth without becoming more complex, and their surrealist implications seem constantly more relative. His works are never thin, either technically or emotionally, and I believe they are assured a long life. He once said, "For me no great art has ever existed without some mystery and some awe. It is that vast intangible, which can never be defined but only felt in an elusive way, that stirs the spirit." Some of his paintings stir the spirit profoundly.

*This last characteristic only applies to the first few "Mandalas" that Carter painted—*Eds.

THE EARLY YEARS

by
Frank Anderson Trapp

It was some fifty years ago that I first met Clarence Carter. I was one of a number of high school students privileged to attend special art classes given on Saturday mornings and during the summer at the Carnegie Institute of Technology, in Pittsburgh, where Carter had just come to teach. In exploring the college's Fine Arts Building, I had discovered the faculty painting studios on the top floor, and wherever there was an open door, I brashly made my presence known. I have long since come to realize that those naive intrusions upon the precious working hours of my elders could hardly have been uniformly welcome, but the artists I chanced upon were genuinely hospitable and patient with their uninvited guest. Later, when I became a full-time art student at Carnegie Tech, those personal associations were extended, and I profited richly from them. Among those who most impressed me from the first was Clarence Carter, a genial, soft-spoken man whose studio I had first entered on one of those Saturday mornings in the winter of 1938–39.

Although I was never formally a student of Carter's, I learned a great deal from our acquaintanceship at that period. I profited not only from our discussions about art and other topics but even more from watching Carter work on many of the paintings featured in the present publication. Such canvases as *Good Crop*, 1942 [p. 90], *Kentucky Hills*, 1943 [p. 91], and *Springtime in Pittsburgh*, 1939 [p. 88], were thus familiar to me from ground to finish. The process of their execution especially fascinated me, for it was altogether unorthodox, even downright wrongheaded, according to the precepts espoused by my other mentors of the time. Where they advocated an overall development of the canvas as a whole, with a gradual balancing of the parts, in the search for pictorial unity, Carter would begin by carefully but lightly drawing in the subject upon the canvas, then spraying it with a fixative and painting it part by part. Although I did not realize it at the time (nor am I certain that it was a conscious adaptation on Carter's part), the procedure closely resembled the traditional practice of mural painting in *buon fresco*. Whatever the case, the passages he accumulated by that process were definitive, and seldom if ever revised or retouched—so clear, it seemed, was the image formulated in the artist's mind, and so secure his technical command. As a result, Carter's paintings of the time attained a remarkable freshness of surface without compromise of overall unity. It was almost as though they had been materialized at will—projected, so to speak, onto the canvas.

The soundness of this way of painting is attested to in the fact that these canvases today show remarkably little sign of their actual age.

For many years I was out of direct touch with Carter, and I learned of his doings only rather fragmentarily, in published notices I came across from time to time. I had gone off into military service in 1943, and Carter, in turn, had left Pittsburgh in 1944. During the 1970s, that long lapse of personal association was corrected quite by chance when our paths crossed one day in New York, on Madison Avenue. We have subsequently visited back and forth and corresponded. When I first glimpsed Carter on the

street after so long a time, I was struck by how little he seemed to have changed. I have a similar reaction to his later art. It's true that his expressive development shows dramatic shifts of mode and emphasis, as he has ventured into idioms that have been regarded—not improperly—as more surrealist and abstract than the realist or "magic realist" mode that first won him wide recognition. The modest hills of the Ohio River Valley have been supplanted in his work by the forbidding crags of the "Eschatos," series, begun 1973 [pp. 120–23]; depictions of recognizable cityscapes have been abandoned in favor of the depopulated architectural "Transections," begun 1965 [pp. 110–19] and the abstract "Mandalas," 1968–83 [p. 118]. Changes of this sort are hardly superficial, to be sure. But in this case they are marked by

an underlying constancy of personality and purpose, and a haunting preoccupation with reality and metaphor, that became apparent early on. It is to that earlier phase of Carter's career as an artist that my own essay in this volume will be addressed. I propose to trace the years from his beginnings through his emergence as a mature artist during the late 1930s and 1940s. I shall leave it to others to interpret the further changes in the subsequent course of his long and productive career.

Clarence Holbrook Carter was born on March 26, 1904, near the manufacturing town of Portsmouth, Ohio. His father had been employed as an administrator in the public school system but had come to realize that, as a man of short temper, he was unsuited to that métier. Accordingly, he accepted a position as a postal clerk. Young Carter was thus reared in a region of the Ohio River Valley where the landscape for the most part still had a rural, Appalachian look, though its wooded hills and farmlands were dramatically accented with the sharply contrasting signs of industrial exploitation—the factories and mines that had enmeshed themselves with the economic and cultural fortunes of the region. In the years to come, Carter would recurrently call upon his youthful experience of that memorable visual environment as a rich source of strong pictorial themes.

Like many another child, young Clarence was attracted to drawing. Although he now insists that encouragement of those penchants was quite unnecessary, his family took a favorable interest in them. He recalls, for example, that he was given paper on which to draw in order to keep him quiet during services in the Methodist church they attended. Although he still remembers his baptism in that church, he confesses that his sense of formal religion has never run deep; nevertheless, he was intrigued by the little cards with illustrated biblical verses that he collected at Sunday school, and through them he first became familiar with the imagery of the early Italian masterpieces that he would continue to admire.

Thus inclined to be a creature of his own personal resources, Carter was not prepared to conform to the restricted, rudimentary artistic exercises with which he was confronted in grade school. Perhaps he had inherited some of his father's impatience. At any rate, he was by his own account a scrappy and independent lad, more given to mischief than to academic pursuits. He concedes some benign influence on his artistic awareness to one Kate Commins, who conducted the Saturday art classes that he attended for three years. By the age of nine, he had won prizes at the Scioto county fair, and with Miss Commins's encouragement he submitted a relief map of Ohio in competition at the state fair in Columbus, and won first prize. Later, in high school, he successfully competed in poster contests, and during his last two years there he drew illustrations for the school's annual yearbooks. He particularly recalls a poster he submitted to a chamber-of-commerce competition. Warning against radicalism, it showed "a cutlass with blood dripping from it and a bomb held in the other hand of a Bolshevik revolutionary."[1] The Russian Revolution of 1917 was of course still fresh in memory. Perhaps a correspondence course in cartooning to which Carter subscribed during these years benefited him in his juvenile efforts. A treasured keepsake of the time is a drawing of a frog done when the artist was six years of age. It is now impossible to suppress the notion that the looming creatures of Carter's "Over and Above" series of the 1960s [pp. 106–9] are already portended in its features.

All of these overtures were commonplace enough for a young person of artistic inclinations, even under circumstances as limited as those afforded in the Portsmouth schools of the day. Typically, the high school program there included no formal instruction in the visual arts. The only adult encouragement Carter enjoyed was provided by a teacher of shorthand, who harbored personal aspirations as a poet and volunteered as a mentor to those students who gave signs of artistic commitment. Among his schoolmates in that coterie, Carter now recalls one chum in particular, a Woodrow ("Woodie") Ishmael, who was fond of drawing religious subjects in which persons "were pulled above their own strengths."# Another close companion was a doctor's son headed for the art school in Cincinnati, which Carter had also been slated to attend. When Carter's mother became aware of this, she counseled another school for her son, lest he be led astray by his friend, who was regarded as quite spoiled. As a result, young Carter was instead enrolled in the Cleveland School of Art, now the Cleveland Institute of Art. By that time— it was 1923—Mrs. Carter had long served as the single head of the household, for she had been widowed some years earlier when her husband had suffered a sudden stroke. Clarence Carter, who was only fifteen at the time, vividly recalls the incident, which was very frightening: his father fell onto him when he was in bed, so that the lad was obliged "to crawl out from under his father to tell his mother to call a doctor. His father died within two hours." Death was no stranger to the family during those early years. "Two sisters died when very young and a third almost died in childhood."[2]

In retrospect, Carter regards the choice of the Cleveland School of Art for the furtherance of his creative ambitions as fortunate—quite aside from its function of insulating him from potentially pernicious associations with his high school friend. Cleveland at that time was fast coming of age as a cultural center. The impetus of the Cleveland Museum of Art, founded only in 1913, was just making itself felt when Carter arrived in the city; the more venerable School of Art reflected the liberal educational climate of the area, signaled by the prevailing ideals of affording opportunities for women and racial minorities, as they had been affirmed at neighboring Oberlin College from the year of its foundation in 1833. Interest in the arts and crafts stimulated by the great world's fairs, the first of which was staged in England at London's Crystal Palace Exhibition in 1851, followed by those on the Continent, from the time of the Universal Exposition in Paris in 1855, had led to the establishment of numerous art schools in the United States as well as abroad, with an eye to the training of a skilled work force for commercial production. Since many who sought employment of this kind were women, these educational developments coalesced with

TRACY, CHRIS, AND SKEET, 1910
Pencil and crayon, 12⅜ x 10½ inches

a growing consciousness of the needs and rights of women as advocated by Susan B. Anthony and others in the suffragist movement. Particularly in the years following the great Centennial Exposition of 1876 in Philadelphia, such interests quickened in many of the growing industrial centers of the United States.

Not surprisingly, the lead in initiating a school of this sort in Cleveland was taken by a local woman, Sarah M. Kimball. She and the other founders defined the purposes of their new school as teaching "the principles of Art and Design as practically applied to artistic and industrial pursuits," and as the collection and exhibition of "Works of art and virtu [sic]"# for the further benefit of its students.[3] Originally associated with Case Western Reserve University as a school of design for women, the new institution soon split off into an independent entity. Men were admitted as students almost from the first, and a suitable faculty was recruited, from both the Cleveland artistic community and beyond it. Frederick C. Gottwald (1858 – 1941), for example, one of the city's best-known painters, and a leading spirit of the Old Bohemians Art Club, joined the faculty in 1885, and was teaching when Clarence Carter arrived on the scene in 1923.

Needless to say, the conservative pedagogical principles that Gottwald and his older colleagues maintained from their own traditional training in Europe seemed dogmatic and discomfiting for a young man of Carter's background and personal disposition. Nor were all the courses stipulated in the academic program thoroughly suited to his wants. Admittedly, some of the courses listed in the reports of young Carter's progress that the school forwarded to his mother, Mrs. H. M. Carter, at 1041 18th Street in Portsmouth, do seem unexciting. Still, they were suited to the professional prospects of the era. Hence Carter's proposed design for a grille for use as a decorative panel, illustrated in color in the school catalogue for 1927–28, reminds the present-day reader of the relevance of inculcating skills in the "decorative use of figures in theatre interiors" at a time when great movie palaces were proliferating in great numbers.[4] Carter now admits to little enthusiasm for most of the formal instruction he experienced at the school, and he once withdrew to live in Florida for some months during his junior year in order to work in oils and watercolors on his own. He nevertheless decided ultimately to return to Cleveland, and arranged to graduate with his class as a major in portrait painting. He now credits one of his

teachers there, Paul Travis, with providing him valuable encouragement at a time when sympathetic understanding from his elders was what he needed most of all. Also a native of the Ohio Valley, Travis was happily more attuned to Carter's natural bent than were some of his nonlocal faculty colleagues. Still, those school days can hardly have been altogether bleak, as a photograph showing Carter posed with five of his fraternity brothers at Alpha Beta Delta vividly affirms.

Most significant of all for Carter's professional future, however, was his encounter, while still a student, with William Mathewson Milliken (1889–1978), who would become an important figure to Carter during these years of his budding career. Milliken joined the Cleveland Museum in 1919, as curator of decorative arts, and became curator of paintings there in 1925, when the relatively new institution was rapidly assuming major scale. He was destined to succeed to the directorship in 1930, a post he held until his retirement in 1958. Milliken was thus in a position to help advance the cause of a young protégé. He and Carter met in 1925, in one of the museum galleries, where the artist was working on a watercolor copy of a recent oil *pietá* by a Belgian artist named Anto-Carte, then prominent but now obscure. (The Christ figure in this painting, the dead son over whom the mother grieves, is a miner.) Carter was spending the days of the Easter vacation in the museum, where he could learn by copying the pictures that attracted his eye. As he recalls, Milliken expressed concern that the student's copy was too close to the look of the original work, and insisted that it be sent to the artist for approval before Carter could remove it from the museum. In due course it was certified by Anto-Carte and was accordingly turned over to Carter, who still has it. Carter was at first put off by Milliken's punctiliousness, and by his fussiness as a client at a tea room not far from the museum, where Carter earned extra cash by waiting on tables. But eventually their relationship became more friendly. Indeed, Milliken assumed the role of adviser and patron to Carter, and over the many years since those student days the artist has continued to cherish his remembrances of his warm friendship with Milliken and his mother, both of whose portraits he painted.

In the summer of 1926, with only one year left of his formal obligations at school, Carter began work on his most ambitious project to date, *Lady of Shalott* [p. 49], which he first conceived that spring. Carter describes his under-

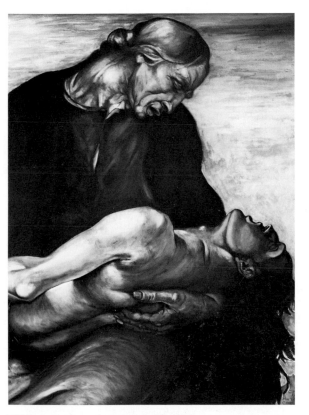

PIETA (copy from Anto-Carte oil), 1925
Watercolor, 26 x 20 inches

taking as follows:

It was Easter vacation time, but I never went home for vacations because I always had some project I wanted to work on. I had the fraternity house all to myself which was very conducive to thinking. It was dusk, and I was listening to the radio. A poem—*The Lady of Shalott*, by Alfred Lord Tennyson—was being read. It struck a responsive chord. I was very interested in death, and the poem appealed to me as a subject. I worked during the summer, and all the while my desire to paint the Lady of Shalott grew stronger. I quit my job as a draughtsman in a block engine plant a week before I started back to art school so that I could paint my idea.

I stretched what was a large canvas for me at that time, 37" x 53". My idea included morning glories festooned over the bier to symbolize the brevity of life, and I had to get up early and work furiously before the morning glory blossoms closed for the day.

Establishing the mood of the painting was uppermost in my mind. Since I had no model for the figure at home, I didn't finish the painting until 1927, after I had gone back to school where several girls served as models.*

Eager for the approval of Henry G. Keller, the most notable of his teachers at the art school, he invited the professor to his room to see the picture. Keller was enthusiastic, and in 1927 Carter entered his unabashedly romantic work for the Cleveland Museum's annual May Show with expectations of success. Unfortunately, though other works of Carter's were accepted for the exhibition, *Lady of Shalott* was not. The artist subsequently withheld it from public view until 1974.

Once his courses in Cleveland were concluded, Carter set about finding the means of going abroad to expand his artistic horizons. By good fortune, one of his paintings had won third prize in the May Show, and thanks to Milliken's generous intervention, it was purchased for the museum collection. Furthermore, Carter's other four pictures exhibited in the show were sold to local collectors responding to Milliken's favorable opinion of the young artist's promise. Thus Carter was able to travel, and commenced within the year. He attests that "Milliken masterminded my itinerary. While I was in Portsmouth after graduation he purchased my

passage on the Italian liner *Duilio.*"* After landing in the ship's home port of Naples, Carter proceeded to Rome. Here he met another Cleveland artist, Louise Maloney, who herself had recently won a prize in the May Show with a group of portraits of women of Anticoli Corrado, a hill town in Latium, approximately 25 miles northeast of Rome. She had taken up residence there while studying with Maurice Sterne, to whom she introduced Carter.

Maurice and his wife Vera had me over for dinner one evening. It was quite a thrill to have dinner with the very famous artist and his beautiful wife, who was one of the Duncan dancers.

Later he and Louise discussed me, and at breakfast she said that they thought that the plunge into the primitive life of Anticoli was difficult to adjust to. She said that they thought that I should go to Capri

for a while to adjust, and then return to Anticoli. A couple who had a studio at Tomasino's, where I had mine, were going to Capri soon to study with Hans Hofmann, so it was arranged that I would travel with them. We traveled by third class and arrived in Naples in the morning and on to Capri by boat. I arrived very tired and had no place to stay. Hofmann took pity on me and started out after class to find a place for me to live. The class had six weeks to go, and he said that he would give me the six weeks for the price of a month's tuition. I had intended not to study, as I had not been very appreciative of art classes. But it was so kind of Hofmann to help me and make the offer that I accepted. I went my own way and painted and drew what appealed to me.*

Characteristic of Carter's response to the abundance of architectural themes he found on

Capri in 1927 is a shaded charcoal drawing simply titled *Forms, Capri.* More surprising within the range of his oeuvre is another, less finished piece, *Composition, Capri,* in which the influence of Hofmann's teachings may well be detected, despite Carter's disclaimer of any derivations from that association. Whatever the case, one is reminded in these works of certain of Matisse's drawings, with their boldness and freedom of primarily linear definition, though it is altogether unlikely that Carter could then have been acquainted with Matisse's efforts of the kind. Restricting his own comments to the practical issues involved in his work, Carter confirms the visual evidence that he "worked fast and directly, with bold and purposeful strokes, using a kneaded eraser to lift out the smudges and add more force and tension to the composition. Shading was kept to a minimum, used only for a suggestion of depth and definition."*

Following his two-month stay in Capri, Carter joined William Milliken and his mother in Florence until they departed for Germany. A fortnight in nearby Siena brought Carter in touch with "a dream city; its art, glorious tolling of bells, and soft heavenly light seemed only for dreaming."* Carter recalls that "the art of Siena was mostly fragile and spiritual." He adds,

Even the many bells that tolled added to this dreamlike atmosphere, which was soft and languid. The whole temper of Siena seemed to be embodied in one painting in the little Church of the Nevi, Matteo di Giovanni's *Madonna of the Snows.* I may feel this because I had such difficulty in being able to see it. It was through much persistence that I finally ran down the custodian whom I learned had the keys, and was able to see this otherworldly paint-

ing. As a memento I have a drawing of this small church in my sketchpad.*

Although he produced only a small watercolor, a charcoal drawing, and a pencil sketch in Siena, that enchanting medieval city left an enduring mark upon Carter's memory, as may be seen in his architectural evocations of years to come. Here one thinks of such "stairs" paintings as *Siena,* 1982, in which his responsiveness to the colors, shapes, and mood of the Tuscan towns is memorably evoked. On the other hand, Carter's interest in this kind of spatial order had already been anticipated in a student painting, *Stairwell at the Cleveland School of Art,* 1927 [p. 51], in which he was testing his powers of perspectival composition. After briefer stops in Perugia, Assisi, and Orvieto, Carter paused for a week or so in Rome before returning to Anticoli. "This time I could adjust," he notes, "and painted and drew constantly." But he also recalls

that "the winter was getting cold and life in An- ticoli was becoming rugged. It was hard to keep my studio heated. I went down to Rome for Christmas and one evening I ran into the design teacher of my freshman year in art school and her husband, who taught commercial art. We decided to take the train Christmas eve to Taor- mina. We painted there for three months. I traveled some in Tunisia and went on to Paris."*

In Sicily Carter had an opportunity to pull together his experiences to date, and during his stay in Taormina he produced a number of watercolors. *Southern Sun, Taormina*, 1928 [p. 53], is typical of these, its bright, patterned look inspired by that Mediterranean environ- ment. Speaking of this and other watercolors of the period, Carter writes:

While living in Taormina for three months I painted some two dozen or more watercolors.

I lived in a *pensione* in the middle of the town and from that vantage point I painted three views looking in different directions.

Southern Sun, painted from the rooftop ter- race of the *pensione*, depicted nearby buildings patterned around a lone palm tree.

The sunshine was always clear and brilliant in Taormina, and I was at my happiest when painting bright light and shadows. At that time, the subjects I was painting were often referred to as abstractions.*

Three of the watercolors Carter painted in Taormina that winter he submitted to the 1928 May Show, where as a group they were award- ed first prize. Reproduced in *The Bulletin of the Cleveland Museum of Art* for May 1928, they were praised for Carter's "brilliant rendition of light and atmosphere, his clarity and consisten- cy of color, and his bold sense of design and

form."[5] The prize group comprised *The Patient Cow, Taormina* [p. 55]; *The Path to the Beach;* and *Town and Sea, Taormina*. Their purchase from the exhibition, one of them for the collec- tion of the Cleveland Museum, provided welcome funds that enabled Carter to prolong his stay in Europe.

This stroke of good fortune sent Carter to Paris, where he again painted a number of watercolors. A new, figural element appears in these works, sometimes with witty overtones, as in *Lafonson's Pride*, 1928 [p. 54], with its ponderous but gracefully poised carcass of a boar. In this and other details—especially in the narrative touch of showing restaurant patrons beyond the window of Lafonson's door—one is reminded of the Precisionist modes contem- porary to the time. Resemblances to works by Charles Demuth and others, however, are like- ly to be coincidental. Traits of the sort were then very much in the air, and there is no documen-

tary evidence to substantiate any direct influence of Precisionism on Carter. Students of the art of the period will nevertheless be struck at the shift of tone discernible in these Parisian works. And though Carter avers that he was attracted to the city only by the abundant visual incident to be savored there, and was not interested in its art scene, one cannot suppress awareness that such artists as Tsuguharu Foujita and Jules Pascin were at the time of Carter's visit enjoying the peak of their popular reputation. The biting, satirical flavor of George Grosz's vignettes of postwar urban life in Europe also come to mind in this context. Once again, no direct association can be insisted upon. Whatever the case, Carter reports that he declined the invitation of Lafonson's *patron* to return to the bistro so as to partake of the roast boar, for which the chef was well known.

The young artist's carefree months abroad could not be endlessly protracted, and he finally booked return passage home on the S. S. *Minnekahda*, a transatlantic transport for livestock. The vessel enjoyed a reputation for an unusual stability well suited to its animal cargo, and typically of longstanding commercial practice, it comfortably and economically accommodated a number of human passengers on its ten-day crossings. And on the ship the good fortunes of Carter's stay in Europe persisted, for at the costume ball customarily held before landing in New York, he was introduced by a mutual friend to one Mary Griswold. Once ashore, this brief shipboard acquaintance soon ripened into a romance, culminating in a marriage proposal at the city's Roxy Theater. Despite the Griswold family's tepid response to the prospect of her marriage to an artist (Mary's father was a bank president in upstate New York), the young couple were married the following year, in 1929. By the time of the ceremony, the elder Griswolds were reconciled to the notion of their daughter's being faced with a life of financial insecurity as an impecunious artist's wife, since by that juncture the hazards of the world of commerce had themselves been rudely disclosed by the Wall Street Crash. Happily, the marriage was destined to endure throughout the busy lifetimes of both partners.

In 1930, the couple took up longterm residence in Cleveland, where Carter had meanwhile accepted a position at the museum. His job there entailed some teaching of special Saturday-morning courses and the provision of decorative services for the galleries, including some sign painting. Occasional sales of his work

provided much-needed extra income. A new chapter in the artist's career had thus begun.

Considering the modest number of actual works Carter produced during these opening years, it may seem inappropriate to have given them the detailed attention they have received here. On the other hand, it is usually important to understand the character of any artist's early development as it relates to his subsequent creative evolution. By the time Carter returned from Europe, his basic patterns had largely been set, though they would assume many variations over the years. He never again visited Italy, but, especially in many of his late works, he recurrently dwelt upon perceptions experienced there. His further travels in Europe, were enjoyable diversions, but they held for him no meanings so deep as those inspired by his formative exposure to the cultural environment of Europe, and especially of Italy.

The works Carter undertook directly upon his return to the United States reveal much the same technical and expressive characteristics that he had evolved in Europe, though now they received a freshly American air. *Sommer Bros. Stoves and Hardware*, 1928 [p. 56], a highly successful watercolor of the period immediately following Carter's repatriation, cogently illustrates that process. In its technique of strongly patterned, thinly washed surfaces, *Sommer Bros.* directly recalls *Lafonson's Pride*. Like the Parisian scene, the façade of the Sommer store in Portsmouth is ostensibly approached head-on, yet its component details assume a jaunty, off-kilter relationship with each other to create a rather jazzy rhythmic effect. And as in *Lafonson's Pride*, the prominence given typographic elements underscores a somewhat abstract, decorative effect, akin to one often cultivated among the Precisionist painters. Since Carter had taken a course in lettering as a freshman in art school, it is to be assumed that the irregularities in the prominent typography are a deliberate sign of impudent fancy. And indeed it is interesting in this context to recall the early pictorial essays of Stuart Davis, in which elements of representation are wittily juxtaposed, with an eye to abstract effect.

For all the resemblances between *Lafonson's Pride* and *Sommer Bros.*, a significant difference arises in the derivation of the subject matter itself. In the Parisian picture Carter is still the tourist, exploring new surroundings with an eye to fresh, picturesque incident. In the Portsmouth street scene, however, he has returned to old haunts, responding to "something

Mary Griswold Carter

(opposite left)
PATH TO THE BEACH, 1928
Watercolor, 20½ x 13⅝ inches
The Cleveland Museum of Art, Cleveland, Ohio

(opposite right)
TOWN AND SEA, TAORMINA, 1928
Watercolor, 20½ x 13¾ inches
The Cleveland Museum of Art, Cleveland, Ohio

15

MAIDENHOOD, 1929
Oil on canvas, 36 x 26 inches
Collection of the Jane Voorhees
  Zimmerli Art Museum, Rutgers,
  The State University of New Jersey,
  New Brunswick, New Jersey

glimpsed along the way," as he later put it, "recognizing things that touched a chord of memory."* For two decades to come, Carter would proceed from visual stimuli of this sort, rediscovering the world in which he had been reared and seeking his enlivening pictorial adventures there rather than in Paris or the Mediterranean—or in the pages of Tennyson's verse.

Another Portsmouth subject painted three years after *Sommer Bros.* is *Julia Marlowe's House—Portsmouth, Ohio,* 1932 [p. 57]. It shows similar techniques and subject matter but is more sober in its expressive character than the earlier work. The discursive, rather anecdotal typographic notes have been excluded; the composition as a whole, despite its rakish architectural angles and fundamentally primitive, orthogonal projections, assumes a classic character appropriate to the Greek Revival style of Julia Marlowe's house, set almost but not quite at the center of the architectural stage. Carter's flair for unusual balances of pictorial design can be appreciated here, as he manipulates what could all too readily be a commonplace motif into a visually engaging combination of elements.

Generally speaking, Carter's watercolors of these years are rather meager in their material character, with their crisply defined edges and thinly applied luminous washes. This disavowal of the exuberant virtuosity traditionally expected in a painter's brushwork at the time was deliberate on Carter's part. From his earliest student days, the artist had rejected the flourishes of execution that his teachers encouraged. Though he sometimes introduced opaque pigments into his watercolors in order to strengthen their impact, he had come to prefer relatively spare effects of paint surface. This emphasis would not prove to be constant throughout his career, but his early oils at least, once he again began to work on a larger scale after he settled down from his travels, would also assume a certain neutrality of textural character.

Ezra Davenport, 1929 [p. 59], is a notable product both of Carter's renewed contact with the oil medium and of a reawakened interest in portraiture. The canvas was painted during a visit to Mary's parents, who had a summer home near Watkins Glen, New York. (A still life, *Plums,* [p. 62], 1930 was painted in the same farmhouse). Ezra Davenport was a farmer who lived next to the Griswolds' property. Much admired at the time of its creation for its striking effect of light, Carter's portrait of him was the first of the artist's canvases to be included in one of the prestigious Carnegie International exhibitions then held annually in Pittsburgh. It won its maker high praise from, among others, the influential *New York Times* critic Edward Alden Jewell, who found Carter's idiom of the period, and of the years immediately to follow, "super-real," or even "naturalist."⁵ Descriptive assertions of this sort demand reexamination in light of the half century of intervening artistic and critical developments, "realistic" and otherwise. Sophisticated observers of the present day need hardly be reminded that the constructions put upon artistic "realism" have over the centuries been periodically subject to revision, as the conventions surrounding its projection as a visual quality have also changed.

For example, Giotto's art at the time of his admirer Dante may indeed have seemed more "real" to the observer than the look of nature itself; but without the slightest discredit to Giotto's astonishing expressive powers, few if any modern viewers habituated to photorealism and its cognates would likely share Dante's credulous response to Giotto's simulation of "reality." By the same token, the "realist" proclivities of many artists of Carter's generation are to even slightly later eyes strongly colored by conventions of their own. The sculptural fixity and patent simplifications of form in the features of Ezra Davenport and of his household surroundings now hold a different, more obviously contrived charm than once may have seemed the case. One is necessarily reminded of other artists' works of the period that were formerly credited with qualities of "objectivity" and realistic persuasiveness, but that now appear utterly governed by convention, despite their clear dependence upon direct experience of natural fact.

The useful though elusive concept of the *Zeitgeist,* the spirit of the age, may well apply here, for the closest analogy to Carter's "realism" in *Ezra Davenport* may be certain contemporaneous products by the German representatives of *Die Neue Sachlichkeit,* the "New Objectivity," especially the work of Otto Dix (1891–1969), which Carter may not have known extensively—if at all—at the time. (It may be relevant in this context, however, to note that Dix was a frequent contributor to the Carnegie Internationals, although by this period of Nazi ascendance he was represented mainly by politically prudent landscapes reiterating sixteenth-century Northern European traditions.) Another sympathetic portrayal that Carter painted that same year of 1929, titled simply *Maidenhood*, discloses more classical predispositions. In this case the linear decoration of the patterned background once again also calls to mind Matisse—if perhaps quite fortuitously.

Carter's other figural ventures of the era are marked by much the same character of expression and execution. These traits are to be seen not least in a portrait of the artist's landlord during his early married days in Cleveland, a work entitled *William Stolte, Ex-Councilman*, 1932 [p. 58]. Affinities with *Die Neue Sachlichkeit* are exceptionally pronounced here. They recur in a more ambitious composition from those early years, *Poor Man's Pullman*, 1930 [p. 60]. The artist explains that his painting derives from a drawing he made while traveling on the Norfolk and Western railroad during one of his trips home to Portsmouth. It shows Mary riding opposite the couple's friend Max Bachofen, a fellow student at the art school with whom Carter had roomed for a brief time. The landscape seen through the train window, however, is not Ohio but the terrain of the Chemung Valley, near Elmira, New York, which Carter had observed on family visits to the Griswolds. Once more, the qualities of "realism" were noted by critics. "The painting was reproduced in *The New York Times*," Carter writes in a brief note on the subject, "and it describes the painting thus: 'A man and woman face each other on green day coach seats, a basket of daisies and red apples beside them. Beyond the window are sunlit fields and trees. A glare of sunshine touches the garish train interior. No color photograph could be so pigmentally realistic.'"*

Carter's imaginative employment of the pictorial device of seeing subjects rather surprisingly enframed occurs in several pictures of the period. Most of them are watercolors, done using techniques consistent with those of *Sommer Bros. Stoves and Hardware*. In *Shivered Glass*, 1932 [p. 82], Carter uses the medium deftly to create a tantalizing design effect that dwells on both transparency of surface and, contrastingly, the penetration of space. *Girls I Have Known* [p. 84], painted the following year, attests to Carter's whimsy as a passer-by in the era of the National Recovery Administration, when for most consumers, goods and services were more plentiful than the money to pay for them. In its blatant profusion, the work's teasing array of hatter's confections, propped up on bodiless mannequins' heads crowded into the display of the Patsy Shoppe, is perhaps more apt to repel than to charm the

viewer. And in its oddity, it calls upon the viewer's capacity to accept contradiction. The same is to be said for the curious views of households seen in passing, as in *Jesus Wept*, 1936, and *Cannon Ball House*, 1940. Speaking of the latter, Carter explains that he

> saw this strange subject when driving through Winchester, Virginia. I inquired and was told that a cannon ball had lodged in the brick wall while the city was under siege during the Civil War. In the lace draped window above the ball were candle molds and a small Confederate flag, which added to the atmosphere.[7]

The theme in *Cannon Ball House* of things seen in confinement was a continuing fascination of Carter's in the 1930s and early 1940s. An oil painted in 1942 is in some ways the culminating exercise of the sort:

> Looking into store front windows has always intrigued me. It is the strange other world that goes on behind the plate glass. Most of the paintings of such subjects were

CANNON BALL HOUSE, 1940
Watercolor, 21½ x 14½ inches
Private collection

JESUS WEPT, 1936
Watercolor, 14⅞ x 22 inches

CHICKENS THROUGH THE WINDOW, 1942
Oil on canvas, 27 X 40 inches

watercolors. Several of the store fronts were painted in Portsmouth and New Boston. Needless to say, seeing chickens in a window was unusual, especially as they were white and all their surroundings were white; only their combs and wattles were red, adding spots of color. I saw this scene in Pittsburgh and recorded it as *Chickens Through the Window.*[8]

Another thematic line of interest that Carter initiated in the 1930s, and continued to develop after his move from Cleveland to Pittsburgh in 1938, involved the circus. Subjects derived from the circus and related forms of popular entertainment had of course long since become part of the common cultural legacy of Europe and America, with contributions from artistic sources too numerous to mention. In the United States, this form of spectacle had attained vast proportions in the mid-to-late 19th century, when began the long heyday of large touring circus companies such as Barnum and Bailey and their competitors. But these colorful and exciting traditions of live performance were also upheld by smaller enterprises, which made appearances for even quite modest audiences along their accustomed routes. In the age before the visual gratifications of the electronic media undercut the appeal of this form of firsthand spectacle, which even so is still glamorous now, it was a banner day for both young and old when

the circus came to town.

Quite naturally, Carter shared in the enthusiasms of this golden age of the American circuses, which lasted roughly until World War II, when a sense of grave national emergency undercut the fortunes of many enterprises not essential to the war effort. Ironically, the national thirst for diversion from the grim realities of daily life was especially strong in the days of the Great Depression and its aftermath, when the circus, along with the new cults of movie-going and listening to the radio, provided a valuable form of escapism. The artist has noted at length his own devotions of the time:

My fascination with the circus and the activities that revolved around it came very early, as did my interest in art. In fact, they went hand in hand. The margins of my school books were always a temptation to draw circus parades raveling around each printed page. I would sit on the curbstone enthralled as the morning sun shone on the glittering exotic world of circus animals and performers passing before my eyes. No wonder that it all had to be recorded on the margins of my dreary school books.

I would watch the roustabouts early in the morning putting up the tents, the concession stands being prepared for a busy day, the animal wagons being washed down in preparation for the parade. I always enjoyed these intimate scenes that were as much a part of circus life for me as were the glamour and thrill of the big top. This vivid living world of the circus captivated me for many years.*

Carter regards *Trapeze Artists*, 1933 [p. 64], as

the most ambitious painting I did with circus material. The subject appealed to me because it suggested both the intimate life outside the big top and the excitement inside. The girls were waiting outside for the moment they would dash into the tent to perform acts of daring and precision.*

The most striking of Carter's many references to circus activities, however, is *Stew*, 1939 [p. 65], in which his fully evolved mastery of the oil medium attains monumental impact. Curiously, Carter's experiences with circus life were not at all protracted, despite the quality of intimate familiarity projected in *Stew*. While other artists of the era spent lengthy periods on circus tours, Carter's personal experience of circus life as an adult observer was intensive rather than extensive, restricted as it was to having access to the rings and work areas of the Downie Brothers Circus during its one-day visits to Portsmouth. Although he was invited to travel with the circus, he was content with the brief and intermittent glimpses of circus life afforded him in Portsmouth. Those experiences, brief though they were, provided a wealth of visual stimulation that long outlasted the annual disappearance of the troupe.

Another, closely related thematic interest of Carter's Ohio years, and one to which he returned as a fully mature artist, was the carousel. Not yet the rarity they have since become in the world of treasured childhood experiences, carousels were a fixture in many public parks, and a favorite feature among the attractions maintained by itinerant carnivals. An early foray into the subject on Carter's part was a small drypoint, *Riderless Racers*, 1935, which was inspired by a street fair he had seen in Portsmouth. Appropriately enough, he incorporated houses from one of the streets of the city in the background. *Carousel by the Sea*, 1939, a much larger work, and in oil, was inspired by a merry-go-round Carter had come across while visiting in the Adirondacks. It was situated by a lake, which the artist decided to magnify into a sea. *Merry-go-Round*, 1949 [p. 95], was derived from the same experience, but in this slightly later oil the modest mountain lake of the actual setting appears as the backdrop. Here as in other versions of the carousel motif, the carved horses are all of the same breed, a carousel model that Carter had observed on this same Adirondack summer vacation.

Nostalgic matters of the kind at hand, however, cannot deflect the viewer from Carter's attention to the larger social and economic situation of the time—the taxing years of the Great Depression, and the disheartening events that issued from them. His lyrical essays notwithstanding, Carter and other artists of his generation were faced with very precarious conditions of practical survival. Like so many others, he competed for the award of government mural contracts, and won several commissions of the kind.

In 1934 Carter completed two murals for the Cleveland Public Auditorium, and in 1936 he painted another for the U.S. Post Office in Ravenna, Ohio—a decorative effort that he now recalls as "an old horse-and-buggy costume piece." His completing in 1938 of a commission to paint four of six decorative panels for the lobby of the Portsmouth Post Office was more auspicious. (Two smaller panels on the stairwell

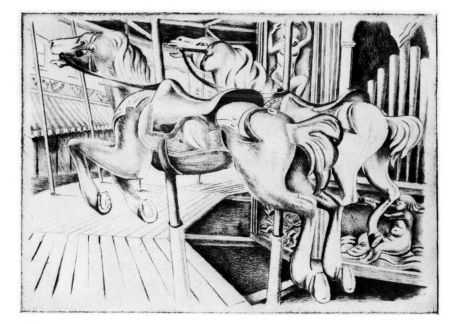

RIDERLESS RACERS, 1935
Drypoint, 5 x 7 inches

CAROUSEL BY THE SEA, 1939
Oil on canvas, 38 x 52 inches
Jefferson Memorial High School Library
Maplewood, New Jersey

were painted by one Richard Zellner, a graduate of the art school in Cincinnati.) Even though the post office involved was a replacement for the building in which his late father had once worked, Carter regarded the project as a kind of tribute to his father's memory.

Carter's subject matter fell very much within a prevailing aesthetic spirit of the time, which emphasized local history and homespun genre scenes—a pictorial fare deemed appropriate to satisfy the interests of the "common man." Hence Carter's murals portrayed the busy traffic along the Ohio River, and the industrial installations that loomed above its banks. And in the wake of the stupendous January deluge of 1937, which had swollen the river to almost oceanic proportions, a large portion of the available expanse of wall was given over to flood scenes. Unfortunately, inundations of the sort were all too common in the days before effective efforts at flood control were initiated. The frequency

with which these and other forms of natural disasters were suffered inspired leading adherents of the Regionalist point of view to a rash of dramatic artistic reenactments of them. One need but recall Jon Corbino's turbulent scenes of deluge, John Steuart Curry's threatening *Line Storm Over Kansas,* or Alexandre Hogue's stark emblems of the middle-American dustbowl. As one born and brought up in the river country, Carter was all too aware of the perils, as well as of the compensatory allures, of life along the nation's great waterways.

Another of Carter's paintings that is powerfully evocative of this mood is *The Flood* [p. 61], now to be known in the form of a somewhat enlarged replica painted in 1976–77 in recollection of a composition originally painted in the 1930s but irretrievably damaged from neglect by a subsequent corporate owner. The picture shows two women seen from the back, bundled against the wind, and overlook-

ing from a safe height the muddy river speeding past their vantage point. A frequent characteristic of Carter's figural treatment is evident in both versions of the subject: with little concern for the figures' underlying anatomical structure, he dwells instead upon their generalized bulk, rendering an effect of high relief comparable to that observable in the paintings of some of the early Italian masters, not least Giotto. Traits of the kind had appeared as early as *Lady of Shalott,* and perhaps reflected preferences formed in Carter's childhood fascination with Bible pictures. At the same time, they are quite consistent with the widespread appeal of all manner of archaisms in the art of the era—most of all, perhaps, in American painting and sculpture, where such affectations were regarded as repudiations of traditional modes of representation that had come to seem academic, slick, and superficial.

Like so many other artists of the time, Carter

Details of Portsmouth, Ohio, Post Office Murals, 1938
Oil on canvas, 10 feet wide

became involved with the Works Progress Administration, for which he served, in 1937–38, as district supervisor of Northeastern Ohio Federal Art Projects. As Carter describes it, the situation was a thankless one. The Cleveland headquarters, located at 4300 Euclid Avenue (near 40th Street and the old Rockefeller Estate) were in a state of physical and administrative disarray. The artist had accepted the position as a challenge, and in that capacity did manage to effect helpful changes. But his reputation was growing—it was helped along by an invitation in 1938 for him to exhibit among selected American artists at the New York World's Fair—and that same year he was offered a faculty post in the Department of Painting and Design at the Carnegie Institute of Technology (now Carnegie-Mellon University), Pittsburgh. He readily accepted, and remained there until 1944. During this period the painter would arrive at a fully mature—even definitive—realization of his creative powers, and would receive due recognition for them.

By the time of his arrival in Pittsburgh, Carter had already initiated the techniques and thematic preoccupations upon which he would build while there. The urban environment in which he had just come to live had its own character, to be sure, but it could not have seemed wholly alien to a man who had been raised along the Ohio River and then transplanted to the industrial metropolis of Cleveland. Carter had already turned to factory structures as subjects for his paintings, so he was prepared to capitalize upon the opportunity to explore further this kind of motif. Even after he had left Pittsburgh, he would sometimes return to scenes of the kind, as in the watercolor *Wheeling Steel Mill, Portsmouth, Ohio*, 1955 [p. 66]. Even after his departure from Pittsburgh, Carter often reflected on the impact the city had upon him. Among the local scenes of his years there, two of many watercolors stand out for their concise, fresh rendering: *Railroad Yards, Pittsburgh*, 1941, and *Stop, Thru Traffic*, 1944. In the latter, Carter's continued affection for typography somehow assumes a different nuance from the entertaining embellishments of the kind in his earlier works. Here one is reminded of the heightened interest in more literal forms of descriptive realism that had generally asserted itself during these years in the work of many artists, not least in the paintings of Carter's friend Charles Burchfield, when the latter turned from youthful fantasy to the sober, adult factualism of his depictions of the urban scene of Buffalo, New

RAILROAD YARDS, PITTSBURGH, 1941
Watercolor, 14⅞ x 22 inches
The collection of The Allied Bank of Houston, Texas

STOP, THRU TRAFFIC, 1942
Watercolor, 22 x 30 inches
Courtesy of Hirschl & Adler Galleries, New York

LET US GIVE THANKS, 1943
Oil on canvas, 66 x 55 inches
Southern Ohio Museum and Cultural Center,
    Portsmouth, Ohio

York. With reference to the comparable environment in which he had come to live, Carter wrote:

Pittsburgh furnished me with much inspiration when we lived there, 1938–1944. During the war years the city had a powerful atmosphere. It was literally bursting at the seams, and I was motivated to put that vitality and vigor into my work.

The powerful blast cannonading from the furnaces was as dramatic as any battlefield. Man had to be there to have some kind of control over this gigantic, powerful world, but his existence was a fragile, shadowy one.*

But it was not the steel mills alone that gave Pittsburgh its dramatic look. The terrain itself had its own special vitality, with its craggy, wooded hills threaded with ravines and watercourses, and dotted with churches and habitations, all linked by a maze of twisting streets. An older part of the city, situated not far from the mansions of the wealthy and the impressive civic and university centers, was and still is known as the Hill District. Even before the

Depression, this once-prosperous middle-class section had shown disfiguring signs of decline. (Accordingly, much of its acreage has since been cleared in furtherance of what once seemed to be "urban renewal.") Particularly in the days before World War II, the Hill District exerted a curious spell upon many artists, Carter among them, for the picturesque character of its streets and alleyways, all powerfully tinged with a sense of human destiny, within and without. Carter has alluded to the character of the place, and of similar localities elsewhere in the city, with regard to his own forays into painting cityscapes of the kind, such as the watercolor *Yellow Blinds*, 1939 [p. 81], or the canvas *Springtime in Pittsburgh*, 1939 [p. 88].

The Hill District fascinated me. It was the choice location of Pittsburgh, near to the downtown section; it had a commanding view of the rivers and bridges and surrounding landscape. But it was by far the worst part of the city, run-down and depressingly squalid. It was in various stages of decay. Condemned buildings had been torn down, leaving gaping holes where they had been standing on their foundations. Weeds and scrubby trees had taken over, and steps were left that no longer led anywhere. Freestanding walls that no longer had any function seemed barriers against nothingness. The buildings that were still standing were like sentinels in a wasteland. Gates, when opened, led into an unrewarding hope of a future. To paint this with feeling and real expression was my goal.*

It should be remembered, however, that the urban centers of America held no monopoly on decrepitude and social squalor, which so many artists of the day somehow found irresistible as artistic subjects. And in fairness to Pittsburgh, for all the bad press the city has suffered over the years, the signs of industrial blight that were unalleviated in some parts of the country were there relieved by the geological variety of the parent landscape, and by the irrepressible presence of its natural growth, which softened the whole. Whether in the budding hope of *Springtime in Pittsburgh* or in his scenes of rural situations, Carter had a special gift for rendering those elements convincingly. He had at an early point shown an eye for the juxtaposition of the opposites of growth and decay, for example in a watercolor of 1932, *Triplet Creek Special* [p. 68]. The contrasts between the man-made and the natural, and the ultimate vulnerability of human contrivances, assume another sort of balance in his watercolor *Storm Over the Greenhouse* [p. 69], painted some years later, in 1938.

During this period Carter habitually returned to his roots in more southern parts of the Ohio Valley countryside, often crossing the river into Kentucky, where his mother had been raised and where many of his relatives lived. *Outside the Limits*, 1938–46 [p. 93], is a painting of rural life in that region, and it was greeted by unusual critical success. The painter has commented on the personal meanings he found in this scene:

> There was a period when I was very interested in wayside stands, as they seemed a showcase for rural America. Many of these stands were quickly improvised out of odd materials picked up around the farm.
>
> One beautiful summer day I crossed the bridge which spans the Scioto River at the point where it empties into the Ohio River at Portsmouth. I followed the road cutting across the rich bottomland. I came upon a hastily constructed stand filled with fireworks and festooned with flags.*

Another reference to his affection for these homecomings took form in his painting *Let Us Give Thanks*, which the artist continues to hold in particular esteem. Painted during the summer of 1943, when Carter headed the art school in Chautauqua, New York, this canvas was created especially for a large exhibition, "Painting in the United States," to be held at the Carnegie Insitute that autumn. (Because of America's entry into World War II, the Carnegie International exhibitions normally held there annually had been suspended.) Voted the Popular Prize by gallery visitors, it was described in the December 1943 issue of *Carnegie Magazine*, in which the outcome of the ballot was announced:

> The picture is a scene reminiscent of the early childhood of the artist at Portsmouth, Ohio. It is the noonday dinner of a farming family, the table being set on the back porch of a Middle Western farmhouse. At the head of the table is the farmer and around it is his family. It is a moment of prayer, with all heads bowed as the "hired girl" is about to set the mashed potatoes on the table. To the right of the porch in the distance are rolling fields, which give the artist the opportunity to present a bit of

lovely landscape in his cool green tones. In the painting the artist has used his wife, mother, his children, and himself as models.[9]

The enthusiasm of the public response was echoed by the New York critics Royal Cortissoz, writing for the *Herald Tribune*, and Edward Alden Jewell of the *Times*, when this and a large sampling of other works by Carter were put on view at the Ferargil Galleries in January 1944. Cortissoz praised the artist's "thoroughgoing workmanship" for its obvious sincerity and its competence. His counterpart at the *Times* singled out *Let Us Give Thanks* as "beautifully painted" and "a major contribution." He added: "More deeply and sympathetically than did Grant Wood, Carter explores the American spirit."

Two of Carter's definitive masterworks of this rural genre are *Good Crop*, 1942 [p. 90], and *Kentucky Hills*, 1943 [p. 91]. The former canvas, relating to another of the Carters' many visits to New York State, has evoked an amusing commentary from its maker:

> Jim Jennings was a neighboring farmer down the road from the Griswold farm. Jim would drive by taking his crops to market and would usually stop to talk. One day he had a load of potatoes and it struck me as a wonderful subject. I climbed up on the wagon, got my study, but I didn't paint it until later when I was back in Pittsburgh. My mother had come up from Portsmouth to spend the summer while Mary and the children were visiting her parents in Elmira. I filled a bushel basket with paper and arranged potatoes on top, and got to work. It was a monotonous job but I made a game out of it, which relieved the tedium. Mother was reading Defoe's *Moll Flanders* aloud to me while I worked, and every time Moll had a baby I painted another potato.*

Kentucky Hills is comparable to *Good Crop* in many ways, especially in the ingenuity of its composition, with the odd angle of its viewpoint and the freshness and conviction of its paint handling. As the title specifies, however, the scene relates to the familiar scenes of Carter's childhood in southern Ohio and Kentucky. It records with conviction the feel of summers in the region, and the richly textured growth from which emanate the sounds and smells peculiar to the place and season. The rugged, weathered features of the two riders silhouetted against the sky speak eloquently of

JESSE STUART, 1941
Oil on canvas, 38 x 52 inches
Collection of Schumacher Gallery
Capital University, Columbus, Ohio

tinues, "I didn't have time. And when I got back, he said 'Clarence, I thought you'd lost your mind when I saw you chase old Jane Reed and Dora Hunt up the tracks.' Well, that gave me the name of the picture."* The catchy double entendre in the title that Carter thus struck upon is typical of the sly ring of many another title that he has adopted for his works. *Jane Reed and Dora Hunt* shows something hallucinatory in the look of the wraithlike pair, witnessed in the spell of their twilight pursuit. It is perhaps of interest, however, to learn that a devotion to gleaning coal was in this instance probably inspired more by ingrained frugality than by outright need, for the brother of one of the women was a professor at the University of Kentucky. (Teaching salaries were admittedly lean in those days, but not *that* lean.) In this regard one also recalls that the plain couple in Grant Wood's *American Gothic* memorialize the countenances of the artist's own sister and a dentist who was a friend of the artist.

Jane Reed and Dora Hunt was among the works of Carter's featured in a memorable exhibition held in 1943 at the Museum of Modern Art, New York, "American Realists and Magic Realists." Carter's *City View*, 1940 [p. 86], was also reproduced in the catalogue of that exhibition, along with a statement by the painter in which he speaks with romantic fervor about the nostalgic associations such subjects held for him.

Many of my paintings have been made near my birthplace, Portsmouth, Ohio, where the winding Scioto empties into the Ohio River. The hills that rise from the river on the Kentucky side hold many memories of youthful feelings—the vision of my mother as a girl riding full-rein over roads and through streams with hair blowing; stories of the Civil War and the march of Morgan's Raiders; ballads which were sung to me as a child; the sight of women in loose, long, calico dresses working with their men-folk in the corn and tobacco. These women are embodied in *Jane Reed and Dora Hunt*, moving almost as clothed spirits down the tracks.

City View, painted from these hills, shows Portsmouth in the distance on a quiet day when the air is still and stifling in the valley. The rag hanging limp on the line, the worn broom, heighten this sultry mood. On the other hand, I have seen the tragic drama of that river—cold muddy waters rising to engulf the city in its violent

the hardships of survival in their remote corner of the Appalachian country. Trenchantly but sympathetically observed, *Kentucky Hills* is a powerful embodiment of American Regionalist sentiments of the era.

On one such visit to his relatives in those parts, Carter went to work on a portrait of his friend the poet Jesse Stuart. Quite unexpectedly, what remains Carter's most famous work was inspired on that occasion: *Jane Reed and Dora Hunt*, 1941 [p. 87]. Toward dusk, Clarence and Jesse were standing on the porch of the house of Carter's uncle, "Doc" Meadows. It had become too dark to work on Stuart's portrait. In those days, it was not uncommon for people to pick up coal from along railroad lines, and indeed Carter spied two women striding along the tracks not far away. He reports that he suddenly "jumped the fence and started up the tracks. I didn't say anything to Jesse," he con-

grasp; residents frozen to the floodwall in anxiety, hoping that it would recede before it overflowed the protecting wall. It was this drama that I dealt with in my murals in the Portsmouth Post Office.[10]

The time was ripe for critical acceptance of the curious but undeniable presence of the "magic" in realism portended by the contents of the exhibition and by its informative catalogue. Chief among those prepared to sing Carter's praise as a notable representative of this point of view was his admirer Edward Alden Jewell, who later explained at length the qualities he especially valued in Carter's work. Jewell's comments on Carter's art published in *American Artist* in 1943 still seem timely:

I mentioned a moment ago that Clarence Carter's work had been varied. There is, indeed, no single sort of theme that could be called "typical." He has painted landscape, still life, portrait, figure subject, genre. His approach has been straightforwardly descriptive; again he has addressed his brush to forms of symbolic expression. He holds even pure abstraction in healthy esteem, though this phase has not yet been published on gallery walls. Yet into whatever category a picture may seem best to fit, his work, in general, has remained allegiant, I feel, to the attributes cited: clearness of intent, cleanness of line and form, coolness (with respect especially to color), balance in the orchestration of the sundry factors involved.

For my part, I have responded with most keen and instant delight to some of Clarence Carter's landscapes, or to subjects (in oil or watercolor) in which landscape provides more than an incidental background for figures. One finds such ample quiet freshness in his subtly grayed greens and yellows. More than once in the past I have alluded to the flavorsome acetic tang of his color, its acid strength. Then there is the resolute honesty with which—if in fine spareness, with never the attitude of one whose report must be photographically exact, inclusive—he gives the reins to unromanticized nature's bitter-sweet affirmations and denials.

Carter's "Naturalism" is not, of course, to be disputed. Nevertheless, I have been again and again conscious of a reticent aura cousining that of the borderline or unorthodox surrealist. It appears to be largely a matter of atmosphere (as in the striking *Jane Reed and Dora Hunt*, owned by the Museum of Modern Art) or of unexpected associations (the *Tech Belle*); or the surrealist aura, if we choose to call it that, derives from a sense, often hinted at, of some curious veiled imminence.

Be that as it may, there is more in Clarence Carter's art than is wont to appear at first glance, or on the surface—how much more, only those who have delved or are responsive to overtone, can hope to know.[11]

Jewell's glowing appraisal of Carter's attainments may usefully be verified with reference to a distinctive category in the artist's repertory that has not yet been dwelt upon in the present essay, that of the still life. Traditionally, this genre of representation is often regarded as the

TECH BELLE, 1940
Oil on canvas, 54 x 36 inches
[Whereabouts unknown]

REFRESHMENTS, 1940
Oil on canvas, 25 x 30 inches
Collection of Dr. and Mrs. E. Vernon Smith

touchstone of an artist's style, and Carter's approach to it does indeed yield insights that corroborate Jewell's appreciation. The artist's still life efforts isolate his special delight in an ostensibly objective description that is nevertheless personal in color, fresh in touch, and balanced in form. Numerous still life compositions, among which *Refreshments*, 1940, or the later, more elaborate *Flowers of the Hills*, 1949 [p. 94], might usefully be cited, confirm that happy fusion of attributes. In these delightful exercises, Carter's peculiar sensitivity to textural, tangible essences—a quality conspicuous in his rendition of the natural elements of landscape—becomes still more salient. Here his performance brings to mind his great predecessor Courbet, whose powerful urge to invite tactile responses he emulates, though quite without imitation. In that sense, *Good Crop* and *Kentucky Hills* seem equally descended from the nineteenth-century French master's *Stone Breakers*, revealing something of Courbet's urge to grasp "reality" as he construed it. Here again, notions of magic realism, and the provocatively tangible appeal implied in its evocation, are exemplified.

Unfortunately, Carter's most complex and arresting venture into the still life vein, *Tech Belle*, 1940, can no longer be located, although the canvas was once very well known and is survived by photographs. It depicts an artist's mannequin propped up in a corner of the studio and surrounded by a clutter of still life oddments. The piece is fastidiously rendered, with a savor for tonal nuances powerfully revealed by the flood of cool light admitted by the skylight of Carter's studio. Seeming almost a "portrait" in its jauntiness of pose and in the archness of its painted features, *Tech Belle* is rather surreal in the way the dominant subject seems caught in a boundary between the animate and the inanimate worlds. It is, in other words, another prime example of Carter's "magic realism."

Emboldened by the success of his efforts to date, and enticed to explore new surroundings, in 1944 Carter decided to resign his teaching post in Pittsburgh and to move to Bucks County, Pennsylvania. Four years later he and his wife Mary took up residence in their present home in New Jersey, in the hills bordering the Delaware River. Carter's change of course was prompted by the opportunity of undertaking works to be used for promotional purposes by certain prominent industrial corporations. The nation was at war, and product advertising was not much in demand; since travel was then

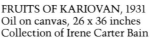

FRUITS OF KARIOVAN, 1931
Oil on canvas, 26 x 36 inches
Collection of Irene Carter Bain

difficult at best, Carter understandably wished to be closer to the gravitational centers of artistic decision in New York. He was also attracted, however, to the prospects of extensive travel in the pursuit of his commercial projects, and indeed his work eventually took him to Venezuela, Trinidad, Surinam, and other parts, to study appropriate material. As might be expected, Carter was criticized by many of his acquaintances for accepting the blandishments of what they considered a commercially tainted source of patronage. Carter rejected that opinion, and vigorously defended his decision in an article written for the *Magazine of Art*, in which he argued that he had not compromised his rights. "I Paint As I Please," his title flatly declared.[12] His early works from his wartime travels include a fine watercolor, *Convoy at Sunset, Gulf of Mexico*, 1944, which stylistically followed directly upon his efforts immediately prior to his change of situation. And for some years to come, in such fine canvases as *Tidewater*, 1945 [p. 92], he would in masterly fashion extend the characteristic lines of the mature phase of development he consummated during his Pittsburgh period.

Among many of Carter's works that have not been mentioned in the present commentary, one in particular must finally be taken up: *War Bride*, 1940 [p. 77]. It is neither an amiable picture nor, for me at least, an easy one to discuss. Yet it occupies an important place within Carter's personal development. Furthermore, it has attracted a great deal of serious critical attention, both at the time of its creation and also very recently, in the flush of renewed interest in the art of the machine age. Carter has described the origin of the piece, and its early history. In 1940 he had been invited to join an official tour of Pittsburgh steel mills organized for the benefit of a special Chinese delegation. Although the Chinese party did not show up, he and his host of the occasion, a well-known city official, decided to make the tour on their own.

The mills were going full blast and it made a great impact upon us. That night I dreamed I painted a picture that was very vivid in my mind. Some of the girls in my senior painting class were getting married to servicemen before they were shipped overseas. This got mixed into my dream of painting of the steel mill which became a sanctuary.

The painting that resulted was so different from my other paintings that I wasn't sure if I should exhibit it. Nonetheless, it was shown in the Pittsburgh Art Association [The Associated Artists of Pittsburgh] exhibition at Carnegie Institute and although it was reproduced in the paper, I still was not sure if I should continue to exhibit it.

Edward Alden Jewell was in Pittsburgh at the time, and he came to my studio. I told him that I had been invited to send something to the Annual Exhibition of Contemporary Art at the Whitney Museum, but did not know what to send. When he saw the painting, which I was then calling *Bride in a Mechanized World*, he said, "Send that and call it *War Bride*."[9]

Tensions in Carter's sense of his own direction were already discernible in 1940, though they are, or course, easier to interpret in retrospect than they were at the time. He had struck upon a peculiar alloy in his art, a balance, varying from work to work, between his creative need to attain a certain "magic" in his painting and his inclination to explore the observable world of natural and man-made "realities." Thus he had evolved different modes of expressing these realities. A sense of hard, resistant surfaces—of *metallic* emanations, so to speak—emerged early, as in *Ezra*

CONVOY AT SUNSET, GULF OF MEXICO, 1944
Watercolor, 15³/₈ x 23 inches
Collection of Mr. and Mrs. James B. Miller

Davenport and *Poor Man's Pullman*. Here the personages seem less "human" than even the studio mannequin in *Tech Belle*, in which the inanimate parts take on the organic, almost sensuous kind of presence that Carter also included in his vocabulary. In *War Bride* these two intuitions are iconographically juxtaposed, but not, in some respects, stylistically resolved. And striking though it is in Carter's formulation, his theme of the machine as a threat to humanity was an already familiar one. After all, Fernand Léger, the Futurists, and the Dadaists, among others, had all dealt with human creatures transformed into all manner of automatons. Indeed, there is a more-than-passing resemblance, whether intentional or not, to Léger's mechanical confections in Carter's own machine/monster—a contrivance that speaks more of the dream than of the actual look of the vast rolling mills of the "Steel City" that were then in operation. It will equally be recalled that in the much-publicized murals he painted in Detroit and in Rockefeller Center, New York, Diego Rivera had monumentalized the conception of a humanity enslaved by the machine. Many other artists of the time, including some of Carter's own colleagues on the faculty of Carnegie Tech, were also intrigued by themes of the sort, particularly those wrestling with the new dynamics of abstraction, the new concepts of "modernity" having posed aesthetic conundrums that could no longer be ignored.

Carter's faceless, doll-like bride fits into this general persuasion. She also has a sentimental quality, however, which ultimately seems to have more to do with the fanciful apparition of her older cousin, *Lady of Shalott*, than with the more pragmatically derived images of Carter's other work to date. As his own account implies, the artist himself recognized this anomalous quality in the picture at the very moment when he had just completed it. What he could not yet know was that *War Bride* was the harbinger of preoccupations yet to be addressed, in future works undertaken in the busy, productive decades of his subsequent career.

NOTES

*Written notes by the Artist

#Conversations with the Author

1. Franz Geirhaas and Brigitte Hellgoth, *The Creative Act: Paths to Realization*, Trenton, New Jersey: Friends of the New Jersey State Museum, ca. 1984, "Clarence Carter," pp. 22–33.

2. Ibid.

3. Nancy Coe Wixom, *Cleveland Institute of Art: The First Hundred Years, 1882–1982*, Cleveland: Cleveland Institute of Art, 1983. This and other information about the history of the school derive mainly from this source.

4. Thanks are due Joseph McCullough, President of the Cleveland Institute of Art, and his staff for making available pertinent documents relating to this study.

5. *The Bulletin of the Cleveland Museum of Art*, Vol. 15, No. 5, May 1928, pp. 105, 108.

6. Edward Alden Jewell, "Clarence Carter," *American Artist*, November 1946, pp. 16–17.

7. Portsmouth, Ohio, The Southern Ohio Museum and Cultural Center, *Clarence Carter: The Portsmouth Collection*, catalogue of exhibition, September 9–November 18, 1984.

8. Ibid.

9. John J. O'Connor, Jr., "Popular Prize Picture in 'Painting in the United States,'" *Carnegie Magazine*, Vol. 17, No. 12, December 1943.

10. New York, The Museum of Modern Art, *American Realists and Magic Realists*, ed. Dorothy C. Miller and Alfred H. Barr, exhibition catalogue, 1943. "Carter," pp. 32–33.

11. Jewell, "Clarence Carter."

12. Clarence Holbrook Carter, "I Paint As I Please," *Magazine of Art*, Vol. 38, No. 2, February 1945, pp. 46–49.

THE
MIDDLE YEARS

Between Temporality and Timelessness

by
Douglas Dreishpoon

We live in strange circumstances today. Our notions of time and history, very different from what they were twenty or fifty years ago, have become accelerated. We seem to live our lives against nature, and time itself has become an abstraction outside nature—compacted, fractured, measured electronically in milliseconds. Our jockeying between real time and electronic time disrupts our perception of art, so that we often seem to experience art only at a distance. We may question the increasingly rapid mechanisms through which an artist "arrives" (nothing is more disconcerting than watching someone rise to recognition one year only to fall from grace the next), yet we tolerate this frenetic situation. We adjust our critical faculties to grapple with its cadence.

In this situation the career of an older American artist such as Clarence Carter presents something like a comfort, for it has the breadth and extension of something fully evolved. Carter's art matured during the heyday of American Scene or Regionalist painting. He has made art for over sixty years, and today, at the age of eighty-four, he continues with his life's work. From the beginning, Carter perceptively probed and analyzed the people and things around him. His sensibility, grounded in American soil, developed an indigenous quality unaffected by his early European travels and his encounter with Hans Hofmann in Italy during the late 1920s. A deep connection with history, with nature's perpetual cycles of birth, growth, death, and decay, and with spiritual transcendence unites every major phase of Carter's art. At the same time, some of this work has a humorous undercurrent, which tempers his lofty preoccupation with metaphysical musings, the transience of life, and the imminence of death. Without humor—a quirky skepticism that constantly questions and provokes—Carter's art loses its greater connection with humanity.

Something about Carter's work has always defied simple categories. At first glance, many of his landscapes from the 1930s—for example, *Port Huron*, 1936 [p. 70], *Hear Awhile the Hum of Summer*, 1938, and *Storm Over the Greenhouse*, 1938 [p. 69]—appear to be straightforward renderings of a particular place, but closer inspection reveals a foreboding aura in even the most mundane scene. The transformation of common sights—a summer sky that darkens ominously, trees that assume strange anthropomorphic shapes, barns and buildings that seem animated and alive—is a prominent

characteristic of Carter's early work. Early on, his tendency to suggest a mysterious presence beneath ordinary circumstances set him apart from more mainstream American Scene painters and aligned him with anomalous realists such as Edward Hopper, Charles Burchfield, Ivan Albright, Peter Blume, and Louis Guglielmi. (In the 1940s, Alfred Barr and Dorothy Miller coined the term "magic realism" to describe the work of these painters, but the term becomes restrictive in the context of Carter's subsequent developments.) For the past sixty years, though the external forms in his work have continued to change, Carter has dealt persistently with the philosophical implications of life and death.

It would be impossible to discuss Carter's "middle period," his work from the late 1940s, 1950s, and 1960s, without referring backward and forward to developments in his earlier and later art. If the roots of his American Scene period issue from a documentary impulse to record the specificity of people, places, and things in time, and his later work, from the late 1960s up until the present (series variously titled "Transections," "Mandalas," "Eschatos," and others [pp. 110–23]), strives toward spiritual transcendence, his middle period embodies the tension between these two realms. Carter's quest for transcendence developed naturally, and many of his early landscapes and industrial scenes reflect his poetic preoccupation with this

condition. Ultimately, coming to the conclusion that specificity was incompatible with timelessness, he began to investigate new forms and symbols that functioned more universally. In its progression from the terrestrial to the spiritual, Carter's work probed the metaphysical implications of death.

An experience Carter had as a child provides insight into this development in his art. In a letter he wrote to the art critic Lawrence Campbell in 1971, Carter recalls digging holes in the ground wide enough to sit in. Nestled within a semisubterranean cubicle, surrounded on all sides by earth, he would contemplate the blue sky over him. The contrast between these two levels of existence—confinement below, boundless expanse above—left an indelible impression on his mind. Whether consciously or unconsciously, this later became an ideological basis for his art.

In his work from the 1940s and 1950s, Carter dwelt heavily on the implications of death. As one element within a greater cosmological order, death was never totally absent from his earlier painting, but by the late 1940s it had surfaced as a prevalent and disturbing presence. In many theological doctrines, death is an essential prerequisite to rebirth, resurrection, and transcendence; in Carter's world view it operates similarly, as a stepping stone or bridge between matter and spirit. Not all the paintings from the middle period grapple with these ideas. Those that do, however, become metaphorical equivalents for the dissolution of matter and the temporal imprisonment of the spirit.

In works such as *Fall Sunflower*, 1947, and *Crow Scarecrow*, 1950 [p. 99], death is implied through depiction of the seasonal passing of the summer and a crow's dangling carcass, respectively. During the autumnal phase described in *Fall Sunflower*, landscape slowly dies; its surface vegetation returns to the earth. In both paintings, death overshadows growth. Many images from this transitional period have an unsettling ponderousness, as though some invisible force were drawing them downward. *Earthbound*, 1947 [p. 97], an appropriate title for a painting in which a dying sunflower arches over the shrouded head of a faceless mannequin, poignantly evokes the futility of aspiring to spiritual transcendence. In an earlier picture, *Great Plantations Nevermore*, 1941 [p. 96], a mannequin holding a sprig of cotton and sitting on a brick wall in front of two brick smokestacks is a prophetic symbol of the end of a Southern agrarian culture. Mannequins appear in several paintings from this period, and their presence is disturbing. Although mannequins

had appeared earlier in the work of Giorgio de Chirico during the 1930s, these figures entered vanguard art as fetishistic entities, debased and manipulated beings deprived of choice or action. One thinks immediately of Hans Bellmer's dismembered *Poupée*, Salvador Dali's macabre fantasies, and Man Ray's photographic tableaux. By the 1940s, the mannequin brought with it a host of surreal associations and sexual innuendos. Carter's mannequins have none of the sadomasochistic overtones or sexual intrigue of these earlier precedents, functioning instead as human ciphers trapped in time and history.

If Carter's later work elevates timelessness by transcending temporality, much of the work from his middle period casts dark shadows over history. Between 1962 and 1965, he executed a series of five paintings entitled "Terror of History" [pp. 102–3]. The compositonal format of the series is consistent: a monumental, totemic beast positioned up front and isolated against a shallow background. In these works, history is transformed into a specter of death and destruction. As animal counterparts to the faceless mannequins of the earlier work, these mythic creatures loom over the barren landscapes behind them like harbingers of doom.

Primordial phantoms, atavistic nightmares exhumed, they are aberrations of nature, the toxic consequences of history's dysfunction. They are cruel and threatening, and their brutal physicality is reinforced by their material density. These are some of the toughest pictures Carter has produced. As a group, they bring to a culmination the artist's perception of history as earthly condition, a destructive rather than a constructive force, and they presage images with more cosmologic implications.

Carter's transition from the 1940s and 1950s to the 1960s and 1970s was accompanied by a shift in formal strategy. "During the war years," he wrote in 1984 in The Portsmouth Collection exhibition catalogue, "so-called 'fine art' was going in only one limited direction, which I was not sympathetic to. I found that the creative things I did for advertising developed my desire to experiment and to become more inventive. This might seem strange to many, but during my commercial art period I became more inclined toward abstraction and more daring than I had been before." In the early 1950s Carter became involved with an advertising campaign for the First National City Bank of New York. His experiments with collage at this time

TERROR OF HISTORY #5, 1963
Acrylic and sand on Scintilla, 35 x 23¼ inches

TERROR OF HISTORY #4, 1963
(The Bird That Hatched The Egg Of Experience)
Acrylic and sand on Scintilla, 35 x 23¼ inches

marked a departure from his former interest in verisimilitude and direct transcription. Collage is perfectly suited to Carter's sensibility; he continues to use it today. In the 1950s it allowed him to improvise with a free-form juxtaposition of pictorial elements. Collage liberated Carter by rupturing the illusionism of his earlier work and initiating an aesthetic based on assemblage.

In the late 1940s and throughout the 1950s, as part of a nationwide advertising campaign to promote native products and industries, City Bank of New York instituted a "famous artists series," including works by Thomas Hart Benton, John Steuart Curry, and Walter Murch, among others, which focused on the themes "Products of America" and "Industries and Businesses." For "Products of America," Carter executed two images in 1948 entitled *The Fruit of the Land* and *The Country Milk Run.* Encouraged by the success of "Products of America," City Bank decided to continue the project. Between 1951 and 1958, Carter completed twenty-five advertisements for "Industries and Businesses." Carter's pictures were reproduced on the back covers of *Fortune* magazine and on the inside pages of *Time,*

THE FRUIT OF THE LAND, 1948
Oil on canvas, 23 x 29½ inches
Collection of Citibank, New York

THE COUNTRY MILK RUN, 1948
Oil on canvas, 23¼ x 30¼ inches
Collection of Citibank, New York

Newsweek, Business Week, and *U.S. News & World Report*. Working with the art director for the advertising agency that carried the City Bank account, Batton, Barton, Durstine & Osborne, he illustrated subjects such as "Aluminum," "Farm Equipment," and "Mining." In addition to their formal inventiveness, his images are potent signs of a burgeoning American economy. The postwar industries of agriculture and mining were perfect markets for an enterprising banking establishment, as the executives of City Bank certainly realized when they initiated their campaign. The text written to accompany each image combines impressive statistics with a healthy dose of national pride. Each ad is effusively optimistic. The bank's central objective was to promote business and industry nationwide, and to illuminate their relationship to banking. "Pipelines built natural gas…and bank loans build pipelines," a typical statement reads, making the connection perfectly clear. If bank loans were beneficial to private investors, they also bolstered the economy of the country as a whole. In City Bank's clever advertising program, individualism and nationalism were inextricably bound.

Carter's input gave the City Bank campaign a strong visual impact. He deliberately kept his designs clean edged and uncluttered, and he selected motifs that directly related to each subject. In *Farm Equipment*, 1955, for example, various tractor parts—a tire, a tiller, a plow—are superimposed in the picture's foreground. These abstract pieces of machinery hover above a farmer's field, suggested by receding planes of green and brown, that terminates on the horizon with two barns and a silo. The ensemble is coherent and readable, a perfect visual counterpart for its text, which points out the symbiotic relationship between "mechanical miracles" and "increased production." *Mining*, executed in 1952, is one of the earliest advertisements, and it is also one of the more abstract. In this image Carter simulated the interior entrance of a mine by overlapping brown and black pentagons. White railroad tracks lead from the foreground into the center of the picture, terminating under a rail car whose storage bin is a bright red trapezoid. Within a pared-down geometric scaffolding worthy of Josef Albers's *Homage to the Square*, Carter created a strong visual message. Over the course of City Bank's campaign, which later expanded overseas, his involvement with graphic design helped to break down the barrier between fine art and commercial art and led to

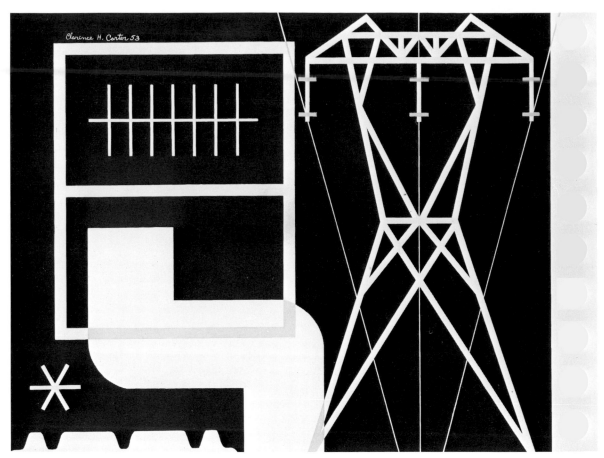

ALUMINUM, 1953
Aluminum paint on board, 15½ x 21 inches
Collection of Citibank, New York

FARM EQUIPMENT, 1955
Oil on panel
Collection of Citibank, New York

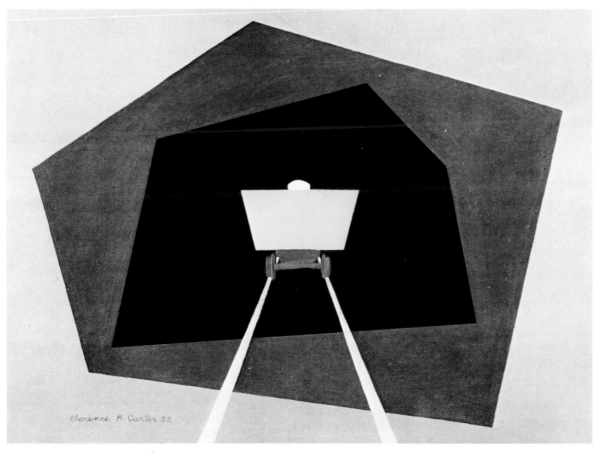

MINING, 1953
Oil on panel, 15½ x 21 inches
Collection of Citibank, New York

PIPELINES, 1955
Oil on panel, 15½ x 21 inches
Collection of Citibank, New York

his further investigation of collage.

Anyone who knows Carter knows that he possesses a sharp wit. This may seem at odds with his inclination toward metaphysical speculation, but in fact the two traits balance each other perfectly. Pondering life, death, and transcendence to the exclusion of all else would be tedious. When meditating on the sublime, one needs a sensible escape at a certain point. Humor provides an out, a human response to lofty, unanswerable questions. It is not so strange, then, that Carter should periodically make humorous works. These undertakings represent a whimsical, lighthearted alternative take on life.

One detects a humorous, tongue-in-cheek critique of American Scene painting as early as the 1930s in Carter's work. The humor in paintings such as *Jesus Wept*, 1936, and *Girls I Have Known*, 1933 [p. 84], is not exaggerated but implied, like an inside joke whose punchline hovers just above the surface of the image. Carter would not devote much time to a severe critique of the American life-style, but particular American scenes sometimes appeal to him as amusing. The number of times this culminated in pictures during the 1930s can be counted on the fingers of one hand. Unlike some of his contemporaries, notably Reginald Marsh and William Gropper, Carter was not a committed humorist; if he was struck by the comic elements of a scene, however, he occasionally made it into a picture. Some of his first attempts at this genre, mentioned above, are candidly matter-of-fact.

During the 1960s and 1970s, humor re-emerged in a spirited series of collages. Cutting and pasting offered Carter a way to relax, a break from the labor-intensive process of painting. In an untitled piece executed in 1961, a putto, wearing a bright red sash around its waist and bearing some kind of Christmas ornament, soars through planetary space. There is something ludicrous about this half-clad angel tumbling headlong through the galaxy. Beyond the work's farcical overtones, however, there is a connection between its interstellar connotations and the cosmology of Carter's later work. As a metaphor for infinitude, the space that surrounds objects and architecture becomes a central element in the various series that develop from the middle 1960s onward. In the "Transection" paintings, begun 1965, space signifies an ethereal realm beyond architectural enclosure; in the "Eschatos," the series begun in 1973, it hovers above primordial landscapes as the final destination of some spiritual ascent.

35

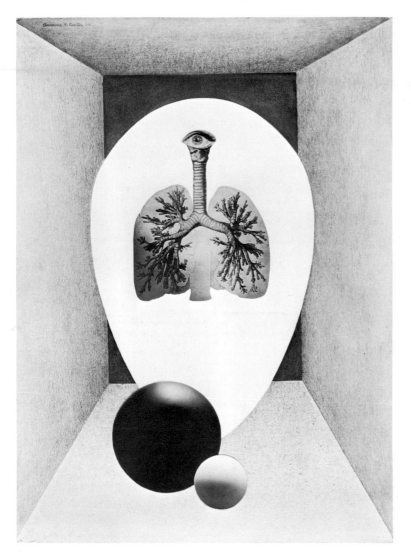

BRANCUSI'S WORLD, 1976
Pencil and collage,
4³/₈ x 5¹/₈ inches
Collection of Dr. Florence Hetzler

As materiality gives way to spirituality, space assumes a greater and greater symbolic significance. In *It's Time*, 1974 [p. 127], a collage that Carter made for his son Blake as a Christmas present, the face of a large clock assumes its place in the galaxy between the moon and Venus. An ancient, sagelike figure, with his arm around a young boy, stands on top of the earth gazing out into space. Pointing to the clock, he makes a didactic gesture, the precise meaning of which is nebulous. It's time for what? one might ask. Humor mixes with ambivalence as we ponder what cosmologic time holds in store for us.

In two other collages from this period, *Air Chamber* and *The Planner*, both 1965, Carter introduces the ovoid form that becomes a ubiquitous motif in the series painted from this time on. The egg form has intrigued artists for centuries: in quattrocentro Italian painting, for example, ostrich eggs connoted rebirth and resurrection, and the prominent inclusion of one in Piero della Francesca's *Madonna and Child with Saints*, ca. 1472, as a pendant

36

suspended above the Virgin Mary, attests to their symbolic importance in Christian iconography. By the twentieth century the ovoid not only carried with it a host of biological and mystical associations but also became a paradigm for vanguard reductivism. Constantin Brancusi's *The Beginning of the World*, ca. 1924, and *Newborn* 1915, as sculptural incarnations of this generative motif, perpetuate a form that continues to fascinate artists. (Carter paid homage to the Rumanian sculptor and his ovoid forms in a collage entitled *Brancusi's World*, 1976.) Carter is one of many contemporary painters and sculptors— Myron Stout, Jake Berthot, Christopher Wilmarth, and Kathy Muehlemann, to name only a few—who have dealt with this embryonic entity in their work. The egg symbolizes everything and nothing, being and becoming; it is a metaphor for life and death, unification and dissolution, spirit and void. Represented as pure light in Carter's paintings, it signifies a struggle between the random forces of nature and eternal timelessness, and its reductive simplicity is an analogue for the purging of everything nonessential. In *Air Chamber* and *The Planner*, ovoids assume an anthropomorphic character—in the former a body cavity, in the latter a head. *Air Chamber* is a pun on the idea of lungs as air sacs inside the body and their isolated displacement within a constricted chamber. There is something quirky and at the same time unsettling about this image, with its periscopic eye gazing out from within. In *The Planner*, an isolated ovoid becomes a sign of intellection and organization. The image comments poignantly on the human individual as a cerebral entity entangled within its own mental gyrations.

Though Carter for the most part has avoided satirical comment, in *Is That So?*, 1980, he pokes fun at the status quo. An important aspect of satire is its reciprocity with the life of its time—it thrives on contemporaneity. Effectively unmasking humanity's follies by purposely exaggerating its inconsistencies, satire takes perceptive potshots at the ineptitudes of a particular culture. Its statements are snide and nasty; it revels in insensitive blunders and gross behavior, attacking the soft underbelly of the unsuspecting. In the hands of an artistic temperament, satire functions as an "alter" conscience. Something about *Is That So?*, perhaps its bestiality, is reminiscent of George Grosz's caricatures and condemnations of German decadence in the 1920s. Carter's characters, however, are stylish from the neck down. The

imposition of a pig's head upon a fashion torso is an act of wanton defacement, and a strong political statement.

As Carter entered the 1960s, he began thematically to investigate a host of archetypal symbols—besides the ovoids there are mandalas, spiraling stairs, architectural enclosures, portals, walls—and to purge his work of naturalistic referents that would restrict an image to temporal readings. A progression toward sign and signification in no way compromised his technique; he retained an impeccable draftsmanship. Avoiding histrionics and wild fits of gesture, Carter has never relinquished the integrity and precise delineation of form.

The ovoid was one of the first reductive motifs Carter developed, and by the late 1960s it had superseded the human figure as a central tenet in his work. Here was a symbol that covered all possibilities, a spiritual entity as well as a reference to the body. As metaphor, the ovoid assumed the same role in Carter's cosmology that the figure had occupied earlier, and embodied the same struggle to move from

IS THAT SO?, 1980
Collage, 5¼ x 6 inches

(opposite above left)
AIR CHAMBER, 1965
Pencil, watercolor, and collage, 30 x 22 inches

(opposite above right)
THE PLANNER, 1965
Gouache, collage, and chalk on Scintilla, 28 x 22 inches

terrestial bondage to transcendence. In *Imprisoned*, 1965, an ovoid behind bars reiterates once again the difficulty of spiritual ascent. Twenty years after *Earthbound*, here is an abstract equivalent to it. The sense of enclosure and confinement in Carter's later work, suggested through nonspecific architectural chambers and portals, not only harks back to his childhood games, but comes to symbolize a bridge or passageway through which the soul must pass.

Over the course of more than sixty years Carter has sustained a pronounced pantheism. Nature has always been a wellspring of ideas for him, and he continues to return to its germinative cycles, and to landscape, as a way of recapitulating his objectives. But transformation has been a vital aspect of his progress. The landscapes he painted during the 1930s, for instance, remain grounded in the here and now, despite their mysterious aura; the landscapes in the "Eschatos" series are entirely different. Craggy and primordial, these terrains signify the beginning or end of time. Poetic mindscapes in which time has been transcended, they are resting places of the spirit, a final destination outside history. After 1965, Carter moved beyond temporality to timelessness. Much of the work he produced prior to this transition has an unmistakable element of struggle, as if struggling with history, as a temporal condition, in order to reach a place beyond it. The struggle was personal and symbolic, artistic and philosophic.

After 1965, Carter required a new lexicon of symbols and metaphors for ideas and feelings he could no longer express naturalistically. When his objectives became metaphysical, his formal language changed. Ultimately, natural themes became incompatible with his ethereal quest. But he retained an all-encompassing notion of space, which became not only his continuum but the vehicle for his transcendence.

IMPRISONED, 1965
Mixed media, 15 x 9⅝ x 4⅛ inches

THE
RECENT YEARS

The Ovoid—Symbol as Structure of Thought

by
Ricardo Pau-Llosa

In an era in which most artists have been identified in terms of one or another easily recognizable style or trend, Clarence Carter stands out as a visual thinker whose paintings represent a synthesis of the styles and preoccupations that define modernism. In Carter the voices of Cubism, Constructivism, Surrealism, realism, symbolism, and Minimalist abstraction—usually regarded as mutually exclusive—are harmonized into a language whose originality rests as much on the daring of his eclecticism as on the depth and variety of his assertions. For him, painting is not a search for the imagistic shock of the unforeseen, nor for mannerisms that can be easily identified, reproduced, and marketed, but the cumulative creation of an ethos whose driving force is the constantly refined projection of the artist's penetration of reality.

The "real" for Carter, as for all true thinkers, is not merely the tangible—it is also the thinkable, the dreamable, and the utterable. He has never subverted or placed in abeyance the powers of representation in his art, and this has enabled him to broaden the intellectual and communicative power of his painting beyond the medium-is-the-message fixations that have prevailed among so many of his contemporaries. By embracing and diversifying representation in painting, Carter has been able to direct his art to tasks that his peers have relegated to other disciplines, primarily the language arts. His aesthetics rest on a simple but inspiring principle: ideas symbolized by stylistic indicators can be combined to form new units of meaning, as words and images are in tropes, by juxtaposing their stylistic emblems.

Carter creates tropes by combining concepts, not just images, and the result is an art that is grounded in the power of representation and that articulates thinking in terms both visual and symbolic. That is, Carter's art is focused simultaneously and equally on two concerns: modernism's redefinition of the relationship between the bidimensional pictorial plane and the tridimensional world to which it always refers, no matter how "abstract" the imagery of a painting might be; and the tropological character of all communication, whether visual, linguistic, or some other sort.

Since its emergence in Clarence Carter's work in 1964, the ovoid has become the single most important symbol in his art. It manifests itself in his paintings in three distinct ways. One is as a uniformly translucent flat shape, in the "Transection" series [pp. 110–19], the "Mandala" series [p. 118], and the "stairs" paintings [pp. 50, 51, 130, 131]. Another manifestation is as an egglike, apparently three-dimensional form, of translucency, in the "In Glory" series, the "Eschatos" series [pp. 120–23], and the "wall" paintings [pp. 132–38]. The third format consists of concentric, intersecting ovoids drawn as looping lines against a monochromatic plane, and is used in the "Icons" [p. 118]. This format also appears without the linear pattern, in images of flat, translucent, overlapping ovoids in some of the "Icons" and "Mandalas."[1]

In the "Transection" series, the flat, translucent ovoids are depicted in hard-edged architectural settings that evoke buildings, archways, and crypts. The use of architectural settings is also fundamental to his "stairs" and "wall" paintings. Throughout his career, in fact, Carter has explored the ambiguity of architectural space —its hard-edged purity (the blankness of walls, the mathematical delights of perspective) and its existential reverberations as shelter, an extension of the human form as social and psychosexual symbol. These ambiguities are also evoked by the ovoid motif, when the "egg" as symbol of fertility becomes shelter and mathematical entity as well. The presence of the ovoid in an architectural setting activates the existential dimension of this image and introduces into it connotations of life and death, generational continuity, and individual growth. Even at this immediate level of meaning, the paradoxes of Carter's symbol are apparent. Rendering the ovoid in its egglike, illusionistically three-dimensional manifestation, he heightens its organic significations. Behind its static, lifeless shell, an egg hides a life. Hatching is both the instant in which the life appears and the instant in which the integrity of the egg is shattered. The being's emergence into life, then, signals the death of the egg. The egg as an object is an ironic symbol of anticipation and potentiality, for it fulfills its promise of continued life by destroying itself.

Beyond the immediate meanings of the symbol are the resonating significations activated by Carter's ways of representing it. In his paintings, the ovoid variously connotes the human face, mirrors, shields, lenses, windows; it is also a kind of visual parenthesis, a suspension of the illusionistic reality of its surroundings. Face and mirror allusions are especially evident in works such as *Vanished Armies*, 1970–75 [p. 124], *The Mayor*, 1979, and *The Gold Coast*, 1979 [p. 125], where eyes appear in the ovoids. The symbol's different degrees of translucency in its several formal manifestations, and the ways in which this varying diaphanousness alternately reveals and eclipses other pictorial elements, underscore the ovoid's life as a lens, window, or parenthesis. And the reverberative nature of the symbol's meanings is itself symbolized in the "Icon"

THE MAYOR, 1979
Acrylic and collage on Scintilla, 30 x 22 inches

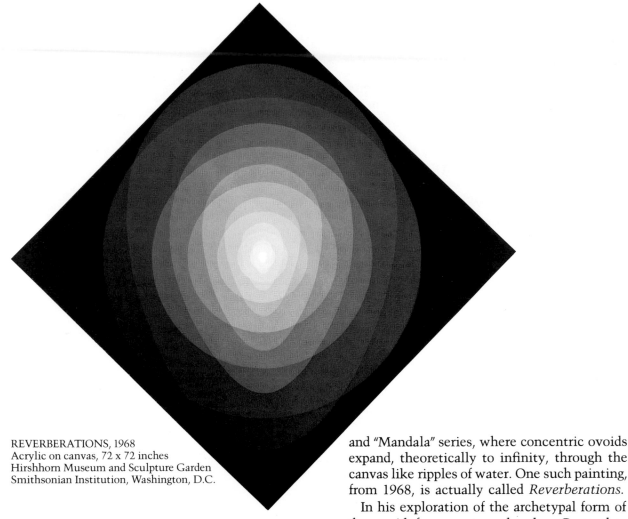

REVERBERATIONS, 1968
Acrylic on canvas, 72 x 72 inches
Hirshhorn Museum and Sculpture Garden
Smithsonian Institution, Washington, D.C.

and "Mandala" series, where concentric ovoids expand, theoretically to infinity, through the canvas like ripples of water. One such painting, from 1968, is actually called *Reverberations*.

In his exploration of the archetypal form of the ovoid for over two decades, Carter has resisted the temptation toward antireferential reductionism. He is a tropological visual thinker, as are Joaquin Torres-Gárcia and Joseph Cornell, Constantin Brancusi and René Magritte—artists with whom he has intellectual affinities. Carter is a genuine *thaumaturgos*, a maker of illusions and miracles, because he is able to dramatize visually the way meaning, knowledge, memory, and trope are forged in the imagination. He is an oneiric artist, not because he conjures images derived from dream episodes but because he explores through symbols the very structure of oneiric consciousness, that level of awareness where language, trope, and reason are generated.

The contexts in which the ovoid manifests itself fall into three groups. Landscapes, which include images of the sea, emerge in the "Eschatos" and "In Glory" series. Architectural motifs such as arches, vaults, stairs, walls, cities, building exteriors, and rooms abound in the "Transection" series and in the "stairs" and "wall" paintings. The crypts that emerge in the "Transections" constitute a peripheral architectural motif, given the particular associations of

mortality with which these images are clearly charged.

Land- and seascapes highlight the ovoid's immediate significations, especially in the "Eschatos," which, as the series title suggests, deal with death, with "last things." This series embodies Carter's most romantic approach to mortality. Egglike, the ovoid hovers above crags and seas, a luminous and serene prism ruling over Pascalian silences and Wagnerian storms. Here it is an icon of birth in the land of death and desolation. But the "Eschatos" paintings also activate the reverberative and synthetic dimensions of the ovoid's semantic field. The stillness of the form is that of human awareness turning mere topography into a terrain of anxiety or transcendence. The ovoid is visually at its most opaque in this series, and also in the "In Glory" works (which have similar settings) and in the "wall" paintings. In the "Eschatos" and the "In Glory" paintings the opaqueness of the ovoid seems to express a density of inner light, as if the ovoid's luminescence and form were conceived as one.

In the more cerebral "Transections" the ovoid is represented as a flat lens, distinct from the arches and vaults among which it appears. Nonetheless it rhymes with these architectures, and is their soul. Except in those works involving images of crypts, the immediate significations of the ovoids in these paintings are by and large secondary to their resonating synthetic connotations. Their strongest meanings are those in which they signify the agency of intentional consciousness. Though they are translucent, these ovoids never entirely dissolve into the encompassing architectural scenarios, but they do not contrast with them either, as the more volumetric ones do with the landscapes in the "Eschatos." The "Transections" are visual expressions of harmony, denoting a restoration of order between elements that remain distinct.

This harmony is the most complex and paradoxical element of the "Transections." The paintings are about the harmony of tropes. In effect, they are visual representations of metaphor, bringing together in one visual thought both architecture's geometries and those of the ovoid. The trope that binds ovoid and architecture in Carter's paintings is generated by a transference of meanings between both elements (ovoid and architecture), and that transference is articulated, in turn, by a combination of two styles or visual languages usually conceived as divergent: the "pure" geometries of hard-edged constructivist abstrac-

tion and the "symbolist" orientation of surrealist or oneiric art. Carter forges metaphors between the dwelling functions of buildings and the egg, but these are secondary to an interrogation of the role of geometry in Western visual thought. The traditional role that geometry plays is to symbolize "purity" and "transcendence," in all the interpretations the two terms can sustain. The "Transections" make ironic statements on these mythologies, and on the mythologies of numbers and "ideas," or "essences," that have been staples in Western metaphysics since Pythagoras.

Carter's geometrism is concerned not with reduction or purification, but with representation, and with the problems that arise from seeing geometric forms as the shrines of immortal essences. Irony in the "Transections" is guaranteed by the paradoxical juxtaposition of the ovoid with its architectural contexts. These paintings, after all, depict an egg, a temporally finite vessel of life, coinciding with lifeless buildings, "immortal" in the perfection of their geometry. This irony is reinforced in those "Transections" where ovoids float in or out of open crypts. A hovering or floating quality is traditional in conceptions of spiritual presences, but here this "transcendental" dimension of the ovoid serves to intensify the irony that results

from the form's intersection with the building.

The "stairs" and "wall" paintings have deployed architectural scenarios in conjunction with the ovoid. These works come after the "Transections" in Carter's development. In the "stairs" paintings as in the "Transections," all the spaces are hard-edged, and the ovoid is a flat translucent shape. But the ovoids in the "stairs" paintings are to a far greater extent true inhabitants of the rectilinear scenarios of the paintings: there is no paradox or irony in the relationship between ovoid and context here, as there is in the "Transections." Different tropes are employed. In the "Transections" Carter engages metaphor and irony; in the "stairs" paintings it is metonymy and juxtaposition that determine the aesthetic and formal syntax of these works, at least in the viewer's initial approaches to them.[2]

Is not a stair an earthly, practical, everyday expression of infinity? Torres-Gárcia, the Uruguayan artist whose art fuses constructivism and semiotics, saw in stairs precisely that duality. Ladders and stairs and all their variants (models of the DNA molecule, for example, or strips of celluloid film) are fragments of an infinite sequence, souvenirs of boundlessness. A couple of steps suffice to codify infinite repetition. Carter's placement of ovoids on stairs or

stairways emphasizes the immediate significations of the ovoid, the meanings that touch on the cycles of life and death. Even more poignantly than the "Eschatos," these collocations address the existential dimension of temporal awareness. Much of the impact of the "stairs" paintings comes from the cool, hard-edged lexicon used to address the most human of realizations: that the finite creature's heroic contemplation of the structures of infinity occurs most lucidly through symbols of things —such as stairs—that are of his own making and are imbued with man's identity as a finite being.

Tropes, too, are devices of man's making, and it is one such trope, metonymy, that enacts the transference of values between stairs and ovoids in this series. Metonymy is the trope involving a transference between two unlike elements that are proximate in some attribute, for example physical proximity. Yet neither of the two symbols in the "stairs" paintings is usually conceived of in terms of the other, or as proximate to the other, in everyday life. The "Transections" can exploit geometric and formal resemblances between ovoids on the one hand and arches and vaults on the other, but no such resemblances bind ovoids and stairs. It is Carter's juxtaposition of these two symbols that generates their common bond, and though this bond is not based on metaphor (i.e., on resemblance), it does culminate in revelations about the similarities between their semantic fields.

In simpler terms, the "stairs" paintings operate through a complex sequence of tropes. The initial apprehension of the paintings is ruled by the idea of juxtaposition, which gives way to that of metonymy, as deep, arcane resemblances between the two elements are revealed. Eventually, metaphor surfaces as the final trope of the sequence. There is no attempt in these works to unite the ovoid and its architectural setting through formal similitude of any kind; rather, Carter represents stair and ovoid as dissimilar earthly symbols of the infinite. As such, they are paradoxical and ironic—both eggs and stairs are functional, everyday objects, yet a thorough reading of their intersection in these paintings reveals deeper similarities and connotations.

Stairs are purely functional, and their function is purely transitory; no one lives on a stair. It is a static structure that provides upward and downward mobility to wingless creatures aspiring to move vertically in a world governed by gravity. An egg—a precise expression of finiteness, a potential waiting to be fulfilled through its own destruction—is the fertilized cell's stairway into life. The continuous process of generational replacement is a stairway all species must climb to escape extinction. Each being's life is but a rung, or the frame between two rungs, in the ladder of a species' historical extension. Finally, stairs and eggs are both expressions of the human body: stairs are a product of our nature as two-legged, erect creatures; eggs, wombs, are the initial, magical dwellings that shape our forms. The walls of eggs and wombs are the first frontiers of creaturely life, the first walls, the first architecture, the first skin. As the similarities between the imports of these symbols in Carter's paintings manifest themselves, it becomes clear that juxtaposition and metonymy have given way to metaphor in the "stairs" paintings.

Metonymy works by establishing connections between contiguous elements. That is, a metonym operates much as a metaphor does, by substitution, except that metonymy links two elements that are proximate to each other physically or functionally, and metaphor links elements that betray usually obvious resemblances between one another. In the "stairs" works, resemblances or parallels between the symbolisms of ovoids and stairs are unveiled by

the metonymy between these juxtaposed, apparently dissimilar elements. In contrast, the ovoids and buildings in the "Transections" are linked by their immediate formal resemblances. In the "stairs" paintings, where a far more complex tropological scheme is operating, Carter has touched on aspects of consciousness deeper than the recognition, manipulation, and deciphering of simple tropes and symbols. These images address the very mechanisms by which meaning is created.

Our appreciation of the subtlety of Carter's thinking here is augmented by the realization that the formal vocabulary of the "stairs" works never digresses from the hard-edged, analytic spaces in which such "pure" geometric styles as Constructivism and Minimalism have been elaborated in this century. The voluptuous language of realist representation utilized in the "Eschatos" paintings could not have brought Carter to the insights embodied in the "stairs" paintings. But in abandoning that representational vocabulary for a strict two-dimensional lexicon in both the "stairs" paintings and "Transection" series, Carter does not forsake the exploration of the trope-generating levels of oneiric consciousness, a domain that "pure" geometric abstraction has often set out to ignore. In North America, Carter is almost alone in understanding the oneiric import of hard-edged forms. Although the roots of this refusal to separate analytic and oneiric visual languages can be traced to de Chirico and Brancusi, artists who have pursued it are more common in Latin America than in the United States; one thinks, for example, of the Argentinians Robert Aizenberg and Juan Carlos Liberti, or of the Cubans Mario Carreño and Humberto Calzada, as well as Torres-García.

When Carter's subsequent "wall" paintings reincorporated three-dimensional spaces, it did so by combining these spaces with the two-dimensional formal language used in the "Transections" and the "stairs" paintings. It's true that the "wall" paintings also reactivate the egglike, three-dimensional ovoid of the "Eschatos," but the emotional and intellectual premises of these works remain closer to those of the "stairs" paintings than to the earlier series. Still, the "wall" paintings contain echoes of all Carter's previous uses of the ovoid, in diverse contexts and formats. Even his sculptures of the 1960s, the first of his works to employ ovoids, are echoed in the towers of *Sentinels*, 1985 [p. 132] and *Intrigue*, 1983 [p. 133]. As in the sculptures, in these paintings the ovoids are sometimes completely opaque, and sometimes set in

niches. In other "wall" paintings, the ovoids, whether partially translucent or opaque, do not hover in the air but retain physical contact with the ground or floor beneath them. The opaqueness and the contact with a surface are perhaps indications of a recent shift in emphasis in Carter's thinking, an interest in the formal density of the ovoid, and in its nature as an object, as opposed to its conceptual and semantic life. The "wall" paintings synthesize the myriad, often clashing principles that have fueled Carter's trope-based thinking since the mid 1960s.

The placement of the ovoid in the architectural settings of the "Transections" and the "stairs" paintings emphasizes the symbol's signification of the infinite. One of the aspects of Carter's work that sets him apart from so many of his North American contemporaries, in fact, is his interest in the infinite, and in devising a system of tropes that will provide some access to its mysteries.

The multiplication of the ovoid in *Transections #1* [p. 111] and *#8* produces a transference of the symbol's synthetic significations to embrace perspective itself. Perspective has always had philosophical implications. It was the Promethean fire stumbled on by the mystics, artists, and mathematicians of the Renaissance, the power to recreate God's three-dimensional world on man's two-dimensional canvas. For them, perspective turned the canvas into a world as complex and infinite as creation itself. It was the suspension of this three-dimensional space in art, and to a lesser extent the elimination of its accompanying mythology (which cast the artist as a kind of small god), that marked the advent of modernism.

The modern artist could still appeal to the title of demiurge, however, by calling attention to the radical nonreferentiality of two-dimensional art. The modern painting was a new object occupying space in the world; it might comment on the world's physicality, and on its creatures' systems of vision, but it did not imitate them. Carter's handling of two- and three-dimensional spaces within single paintings, in the ovoid sequences of the "Transection" series, for example, indicates his ambition to bring the Renaissance and the modernist spaces into harmony.

In this sense, then, the handling of perspective and the copresence of two- and three-dimensional spaces in numerous of Carter's paintings can be read as reflections of a desire to transcend modernism's dismissal of three-dimensional space while at the same time

TRANSECTION #8, 1970,
Acrylic on canvas, 78 x 60 inches
Private collection

TRANSECTION #18, 1972
Acrylic on canvas, 78 x 60 inches
The Corcoran Gallery of Art, Washington, D.C.

recognizing the nonmimetic objectivity of painted representation. Just as Carter implodes different kinds of tropes, so he implodes conflicting spatial premises in painting. After all, in many of the paintings involving ovoid sequences, the ovoids represented are flat planes through which other ovoids and the Renaissance metrics of their contexts are perceived as extending to infinity.

The "Icons" and "Mandalas" unveil another dimension of the ovoid sequence as a symbolic representation of the infinite. In these series, alternating horizontal and vertical ovoids overlap. Generally speaking, the "Mandalas" make use of the flat, lens format of the "Transections," while the "Icons" utilize only outlines of the ovoid against a monochromatic plane. Both series employ perspective to depict exponentially larger ovoids extending outward from the center to the edge of the canvas and, conceptually at least, beyond to infinity. These reverberating forms conjure the infinite through number, pattern, and perspective.

The concentric ovoids in the "Icons" and the "Mandalas" achieve effects similar to those obtained by Torres-Gárcia with grids and ladders, the two structural principles of his paintings. Each ovoid in these series of Carter's is a rung in a pattern that could extend to infinity. One thinks also of Brancusi's potentially infinite columns made of repeated forms, of Nietzsche's idea of eternal recurrence, of the traceries and mosaics of the Alhambra, of Pythagoras and Jorge Luis Borges—in other words, of the centuries-old use of pattern and repetition as symbols of the infinite.

As in the "Transections" and "stairs" paintings, in the "Icons" and the "Mandalas" there is a semantics to the use of perspective and pattern, and this semantics highlights the importance of simultaneity and implosion in Carter's visual thinking since the mid 1960s. Simultaneity and implosion lie at the core of the way he conceives his symbols and contexts, and the way he produces visual utterances with them, for Carter's thinking is linguistic in structure—a fact that enables him to elaborate philosophical statements in his painting that are out of the reach of many of his contemporaries. Those artists who focus on detonating representation, in order to mine either the medium or the ephemeral spectacle of painting for their supposed purities, are more often than not left with the rubble of tautology: painting is paint, for example. Carter's work brings the viewer not to a blind-alley encounter with a medium, but to a confrontation with a frightening side of

human life, language's dark gift to man—the ability to conceive of the infinite through symbols. It is man's bitter glory to taste of the infinite through his mastery over symbols and their boundless possibilities, and at the same time to know death; Carter's work leads one to ponder this relationship between our inexhaustible signs, their inexhaustible signification of "the infinite," and human mortality.

Simultaneity and implosion in Carter's art correspond to the principles that Roman Jakobson identified as driving language—selection and contiguity.[3] All the words that coexist in one paradigm are simultaneously eligible for selection wherever that paradigm arises in the flow of language, and all the words selected to form a sentence must implode to become a complete thought. It is simultaneity and implosion, selection and contiguity, that give structure to a sign system such as language, which is otherwise limitless in its expressive or referential potential—a limitlessness that allows it and the symbols it employs in constituting individual utterances to become embodiments of the infinite. In visual language, the ovoid is one such symbol.

Carter understands that the infinite is expressed in language through semantic simultaneity and syntactic implosion and contiguity, and his understanding is reflected in the constancy of his symbols and the diversity of meanings they convey. He also realizes that the language is inexhaustible because its essential signified is time. All symbols and sign systems in the end address time, for the human apprehension of symbols occurs on the same levels of awareness where time itself is sensed and understood. The apprehension of the ovoid in Carter's work, for example, necessitates not only an apprehension of the simultaneous levels of meaning in the symbol—its immediate, reverberative, and synthetic significations—but also an ability to grasp the context of these significations, the visual syntax in which they appear. Semantics is the product of simultaneity, of a *present* expanded by a variety of references; syntax is a product of a *sequence*, and as such it is the very structure of temporal awareness. Thus time is inseparable from symbolizaton. Carter's mastery over symbol, context, and their interaction suggests his awareness of these issues.

The apprehension of the ovoid in Carter's work, like the apprehension of all symbols and tropes, activates a kind of cognition different from that of everyday perception. To perceive an egg in the world, one need not engage

thought patterns that fuse simultaneity and contiguity, copresence and sequence, unless one chooses to charge that everyday experience of an object with symbolic life. But the grasping of symbols in representations offers no such choice: one must activate these patterns of consciousness or miss the chance for aesthetic experience. Carter has mastered these patterns of awareness, and in this mastery over the way we grasp tropes and symbols lies the key to his rebellion against time and the limits it sets on human life. His is also a rebellion against the limits put on human consciousness by a univocal art that favors reductionism and the cult of the medium. Such art is absolutely unable to express any deep idea about time and existence, let alone to transcend the structures of awareness that often make everyday, objective experiences numbing rehearsals of death.

While the symbol of the ovoid has embodied Carter's ideas about existence, and his rebelliousness, for the last 24 years, it is light that indicates what aspects of the symbol's semantic field obtain in different contexts. The interaction of the ovoid and the other elements in a painting, including the scenarios or contexts in which the ovoid appears, is mediated by translucency—light's fusion with matter. And translucency is itself an age-old symbol of the presence of the spiritual in the tangible world.

It is not entirely self-evident why light should be the ancient symbol of the spirit. We see the tangible things of the world by means of the actions of light on things and on our optical faculties; light is a physical force, in other words, and without it there would be no visible world, no visual expression of tangibility. That light should have come to symbolize the intangible, ideal world of the spirit, and to do so almost universally, is no small source of wonder.

Carter's paintings reveal an awareness of the paradoxes involved in light symbolism, and also a recognition that translucency rather than light itself should be the focus of a symbolism of the spiritual. Translucency results from the intersection of light and matter, or, more precisely, from the imperfect passage of light through an object. Translucency is matter and light combined together. It cannot be conceived solely in terms of either. It is very much like metaphor, metonymy, or any other trope that combines two elements in an indissoluble unity. The translucent object is the phenomenological symbol of spiritualized matter, the symbol of the agency of the spiritual in the only domain in which it can be conceived—the sensorial. As a beam of energy, light itself cannot symbolize the resolution of Plato's quandary of how to reconcile the intangibility of the *eide*—the platonic *ideas* of forms—with their role as the preexisting causes of the tangible. It must be remembered that "spirit" is perceived as the "idea" that generates intelligence (*nous*), and that, as such, spirit is the *idea* that causes thought (*logos*) and action (*energeia*).

Thought is a representation (*eikon* or icon, "reflection") of the spirit, and as such it must be made manifest to the senses. There is no such thing as a representation that is not sensorial. Translucency represents the interpenetration of *idea* and *icon*. Ultimately, Carter's translucent ovoid is the symbol of consciousness because its translucency alters whatever is glimpsed through it, much as consciousness alters what it focuses on. The world is what is perceived, and while one can speculate on a "pure" or ideal world of platonic forms beyond the reach of the senses, it cannot be known or imagined. The various levels of translucency in Carter's ovoids signify the diverse workings of consciousness. In this regard, the ovoid becomes a symbol of more than the dynamics of awareness and the agency of consciousness. It becomes a symbol of representation itself—a metasymbol.

From this standpoint, it is possible more incisively to assess the nature of Carter's rebellion against the ultimate concern of consciousness—that is, death. The "a priorist" model of consciousness that Kant conceived and Husserl perpetuated reconciles man to the perimeters of his consciousness; all perimeters, all negations, evoke death. The ovoid, on the other hand, is at the immediate level a symbol of life and continuity. At reverberative and synthetic levels of meaning it becomes the lens that signifies our intentional grasp of the world. As the symbol of our presence in the world, it hovers in the domains that it structures, thereby giving conscious "being" to them. That structuring, that agency of the ovoid as symbol of consciousness, is itself signified by translucency.

It is translucency that discloses how the ovoid's immediate significations as a life force are collapsed into its reverberative and synthetic significations. In Plato's *Dialogues* we witness time and again the struggles of Socrates to reason out the tangibility of the idea, the presence of the eternal, in a flawed and mortal world of constant flux. Carter's translucent ovoids, icons of matter fusing with light, are an expression of the *zoön noeton* of the *Timaeus* (30c–d), the "intelligible living beings" that are perceived as *eide* becoming flesh. As the symbol of consciousness, the ovoid in Carter's work reveals itself as the point of intersection and coexistence of the finite and the infinite. The ovoid as metasymbol and as icon of consciousness is also the symbol of language, the point where sequence and present meet, where light and matter join, where death and birth are copresent, where idea becomes representation. Man is consciousness. He is aware of himself as matter charged with spirit, and as a being aware simultaneously of death and the infinite. Carter's use of the ovoid embraces these paradoxes of human Being, and in this embrace, carried out through symbols, lies the celebration of his rebelliousness and his artistry.

NOTES

1. The different series and groups of related paintings in which the ovoid appears, and the years during which they were realized, are "Transections," begun 1965; "Mandalas," 1968–83; "Chimera," 1972–74; "In Glory," 1973–75; "Pilgrimage," 1973–75; "Eschatos," begun 1973; the "stairs" paintings, 1980–82; and the "wall" paintings, 1983–87.

   Between 1964 and 1966 Carter also worked on sculptures that employed ovoids, and between 1965 and 1985 he realized numerous collages using this symbol.

2. A metaphor is a trope that joins two ideas or objects by virtue of a resemblance that is posited between them. In his "Ode to Fire," for example, Pablo Neruda calls fire "the pollen of metals," thus banking on similarities—in color, ability to spread, relationship to wind, and ability to transform matter—between pollen and fire in order to generate a convincing analogy. Metaphor is fundamentally an analogy. Metonymy is a trope that also formulates a substitution between two elements, but does not base this substitution on resemblance. When we say that the White House has issued a statement, it is understood that the President or one of his spokesmen has made the declaration, not the building of the White House itself. Metonymy substitutes "White House" for "President," since the two elements are functionally related, and are thought of as having a physical proximity to each other.

3. Roman Jakobson, *Fundamentals of Language*, included in his *Selected Writings* (The Hague: Mouton, 1974). The "axes" or "poles" that Jakobson uses in an innovative way are derived from the linguistics of Saussure, among others, before him. See also Elmar Holenstein, *Roman Jakobson's Approach to Language: Phenomenological Structuralism* (Bloomington & London: Indiana University Press, 1976), perhaps the best study of Jakobson's theories to date.

Oils, Acrylics, Watercolors, and Collages

LADY OF SHALOTT, 1927
Oil on canvas, 37¼ x 53½ inches
Courtesy of Hirschl & Adler Gallery, New York

STAIRWELL AT THE CLEVELAND SCHOOL
    OF ART, 1927
Oil on canvas, 24¹/₈ x 16¹/₈ inches
Private collection

(opposite)

LABYRINTHINE, 1982
Acrylic on canvas, 78 x 60 inches

TAORMINA, SICILY, 1928
Watercolor, 20½ x 13¾ inches
Collection of Mr. and Mrs. Jerome Pusterlink,
   New York

(*opposite*)
SOUTHERN SUN, TAORMINA, 1928
Watercolor, 20 x 13⅝ inches

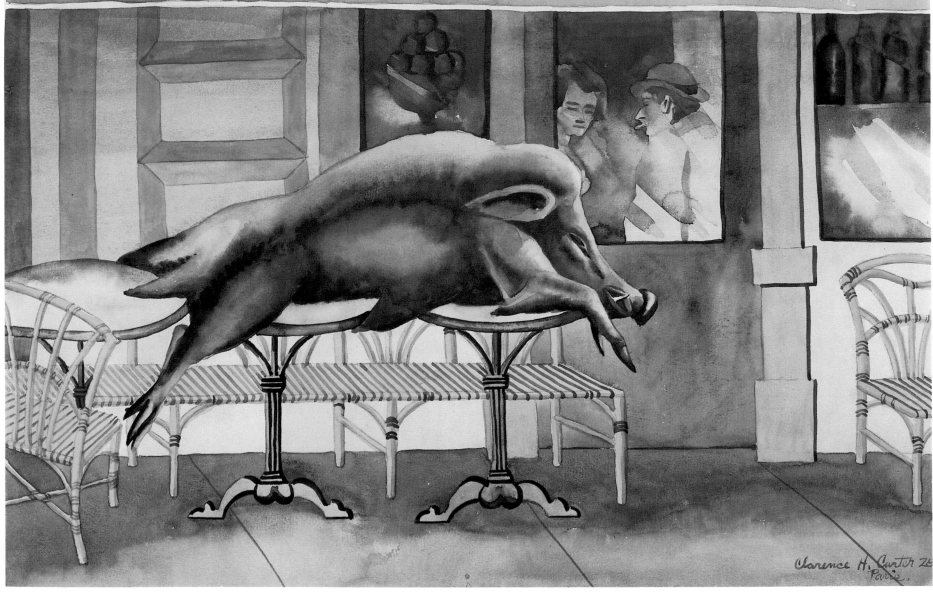

LAFONSON'S PRIDE, 1928
Watercolor, 13 x 16¹/₈ inches

54

THE PATIENT COW, TAORMINA, 1928
Watercolor, 13 5/8 x 20½ inches
The Cleveland Museum of Art, Cleveland, Ohio
Purchase from the J. H. Wade Fund

POOR MAN'S PULLMAN, 1930
Oil on canvas, 36 x 44¼ inches
Philadelphia Museum of Art, Philadelphia, Pennsylvania
Edith H. Bell Fund

THE FLOOD, 1976 – 77
Oil on canvas, 40 x 50 inches
Courtesy of ACA Galleries, New York

PLUMS, 1930
Oil on canvas, 21½ x 14½ inches
Private collection

(opposite)
THE BALCONY
Oil on canvas, 43 x 42 inches
Collection of Max Weitzenhoffer

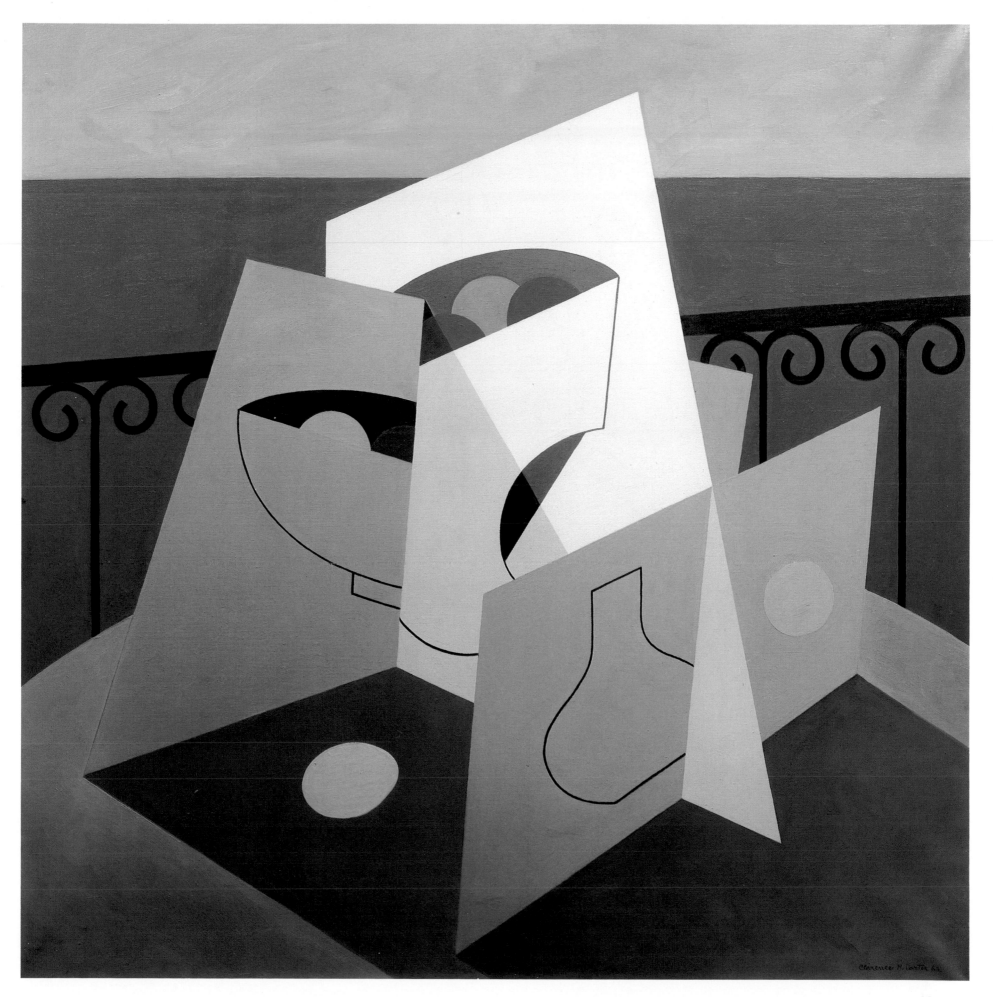

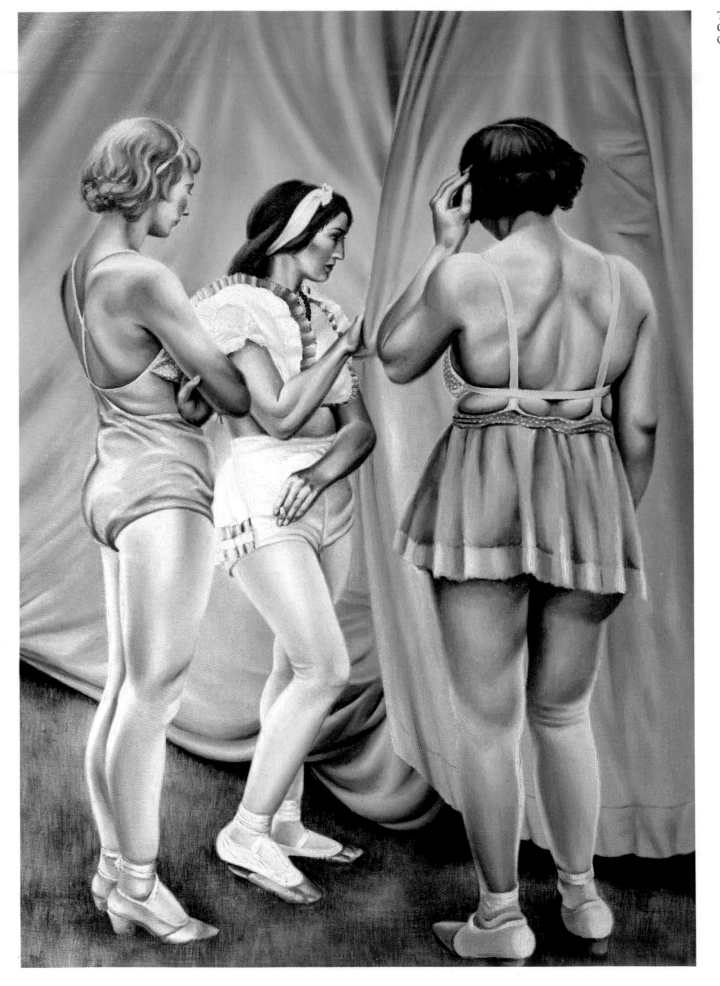

TRAPEZE ARTISTS, 1933
Oil on canvas, 54 x 38 inches
Courtesy of Hirschl & Adler Galleries,
  New York

(opposite)
STEW, 1939
Oil on canvas, 45 x 36 inches
The Toledo Museum of Art,
  Toledo, Ohio
Elizabeth C. Mau Bequest Fund

WHEELING STEEL MILL, PORTSMOUTH, OHIO, 1955
Watercolor, 15 x 23 inches
Southern Ohio Museum and Cultural Center, Portsmouth, Ohio

66

FAIRPORT, 1934
Oil on canvas, 30 x 40 inches
New Jersey State Museum, Trenton, New Jersey

TRIPLET CREEK SPECIAL, 1932
Watercolor, 14¾ x 22 inches
Courtesy of Hirschl & Adler Galleries, New York

STORM OVER THE GREENHOUSE, 1938
Watercolor, 14¾ x 22 inches
Courtesy of Hirschl & Adler Galleries, New York

PORT HURON, 1936
Oil on canvas, 27 x 32 inches
The Cleveland Museum of Art, Cleveland, Ohio
The Hinman B. Hurlbut Collection

70

CREEPERS, 1935
Oil on canvas, 25 x 30 inches
The Metropolitan Museum of Art, New York

THE GUARDIAN ANGEL, 1936
Watercolor, 21½ x 14½ inches
Whitney Museum of American Art,
New York

MACUTO MANNEKIN, 1946
Watercolor, 15¼ x 22¾ inches

END OF THE MINE, 1939
Oil on canvas, 26 x 40 inches
Arnot Art Museum, Elmira, New York

(*opposite*)
SMOLDERING FIRES, 1941
Oil on canvas, 45 x 36 inches
Courtesy of Hirschl & Adler Galleries, New york

COAL DOCKS AT SUPERIOR, 1939
Oil on canvas, 18 x 30 inches
Courtesy of Harmon-Meek Gallery, Naples, Florida

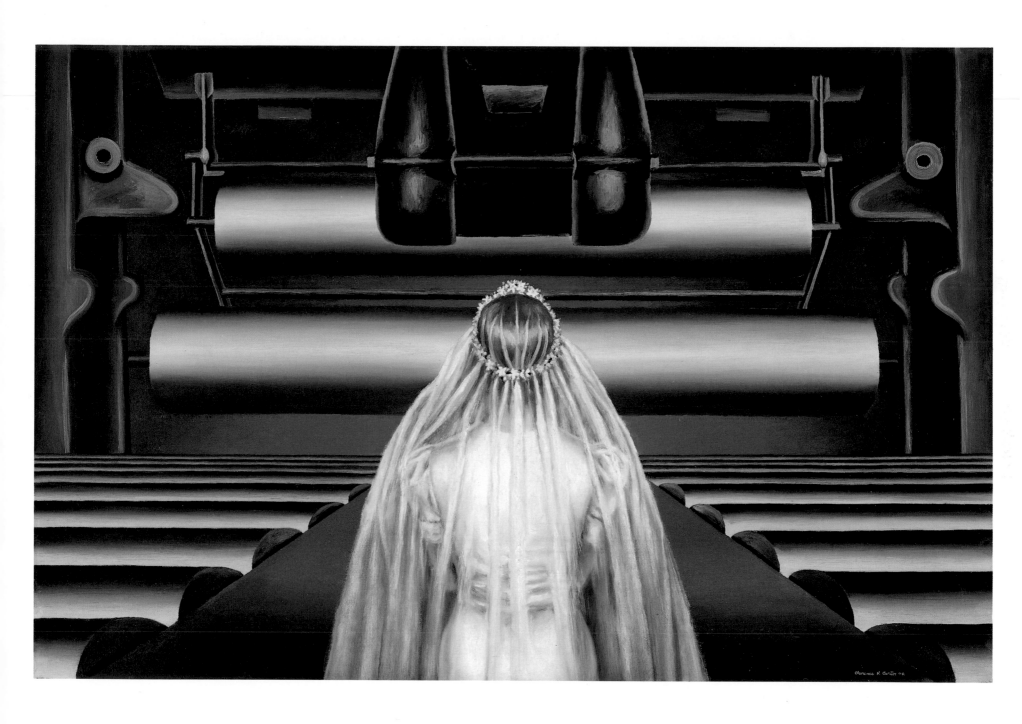

WAR BRIDE, 1940
Oil on canvas, 36 x 54 inches
The Carnegie Museum of Art, Pittsburgh
Richard M. Scaife American Painting Fund
  and Paintings, Acquisition Fund, 1982

BLAST FURNACE, PITTSBURGH, 1956
Watercolor, 8 x 10½ inches
Courtesy of Hirschl & Adler Galleries, New York

WILLIAM M. MILLIKEN AT THE CENTURY OF PROGRESS, CHICAGO, 1940
Oil on canvas, 29¹/₈ x 43¹/₈ inches
Collection of Barbara Mathas Gallery

PITTSBURGH HILL DISTRICT, 1940
Watercolor, 14 7/8 x 22¼ inches
Courtesy of Hirsch & Adler Galleries, New York

YELLOW BLINDS, 1939
Watercolor, 14 x 21 inches
The Butler Institute of American Art, Youngstown, Ohio

NIGHT CARNIVAL, 1941
Watercolor, 22 x 15 inches

GIRLS I HAVE KNOWN, 1933
Watercolor, 14¾ x 22 inches
Collection of Mr. and Mrs. Jean Pigozzi, New York

(*opposite*)
HOSPITALITIES LONG PAST, 1941
Oil on canvas, 32¼ x 22⅛ inches
Courtesy of Hirschl & Adler Galleries, New York

CITY VIEW, 1940
Oil on canvas, 36 x 45 inches
Sheldon Swope Art Gallery, Terre Haute, Indiana

JANE REED AND DORA HUNT, 1941
Oil on canvas, 36 x 45 inches
The Museum of Modern Art, New York

FLOWERS OF THE HILLS, 1949
Oil on canvas, 34 x 46 inches
Collection of Towne Bannon

MERRY-GO-ROUND, 1949
Oil on canvas, 21½ x 32¼ inches
Collection of Mr. and Mrs. James B. Miller

CROW SCARECROW, 1950 – 51
Oil on canvas, 36 x 45 inches
Courtesy of ACA Galleries, New York

OVER AND ABOVE #13, 1964, Oil on canvas, 75 x 77 inches

OVER AND ABOVE #21, 1967, Oil on canvas, 75 x 77 inches

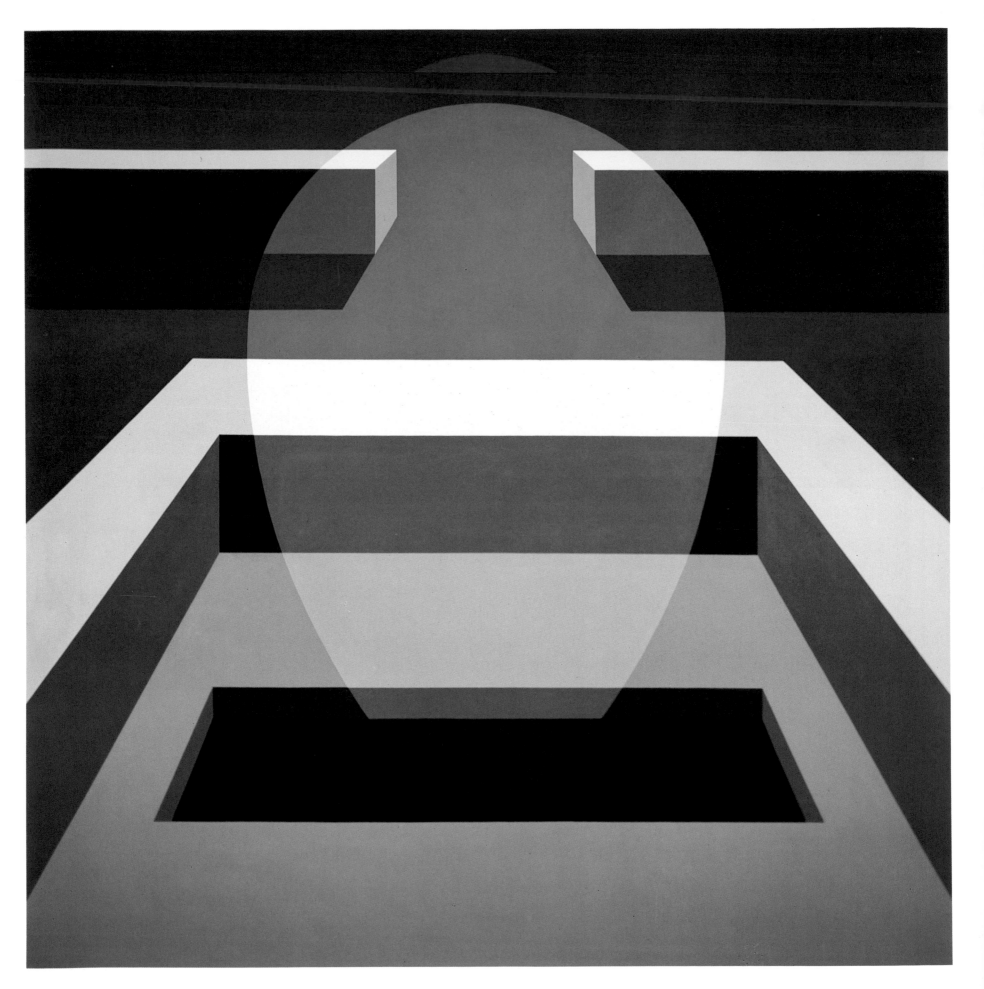

TRANSECTION #1, 1966
Acrylic on canvas, 77 x 54 inches
The Newark Museum, Newark,
    New Jersey

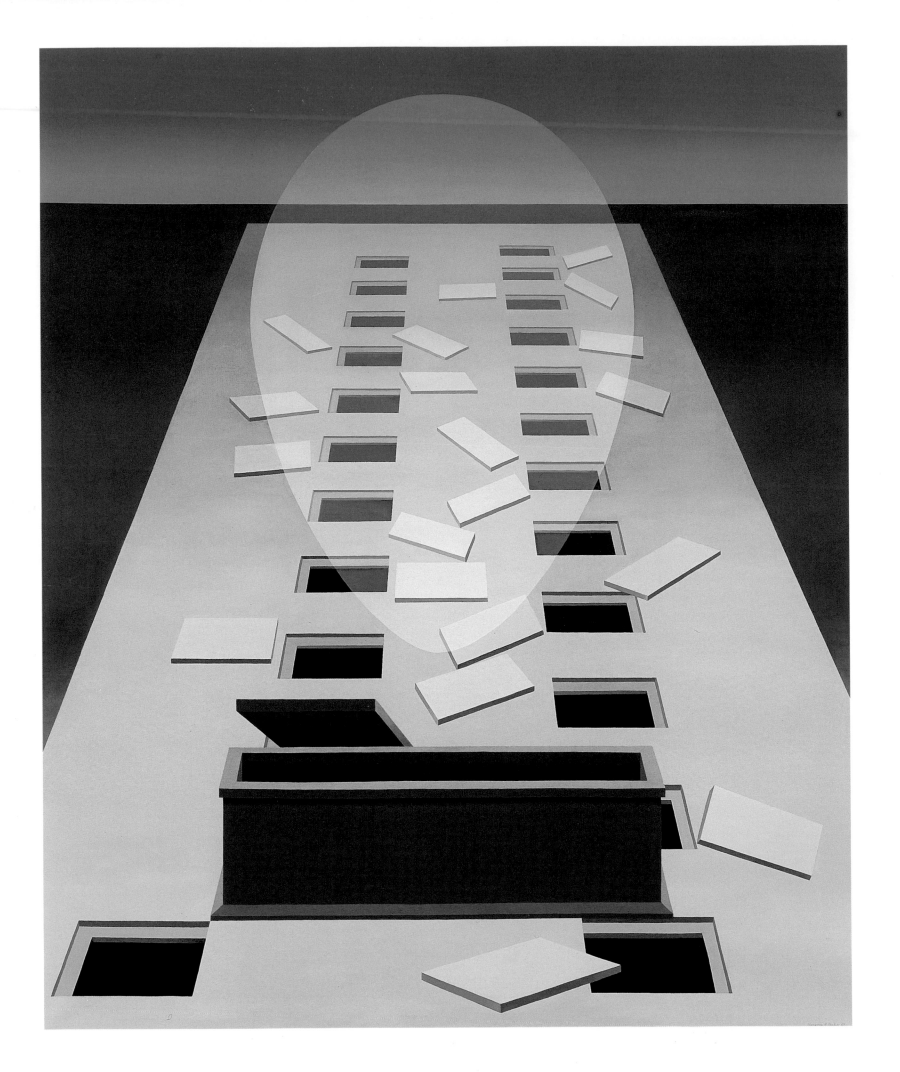

TRANSECTION #3, AFTER FRA ANGELICO, 1967
Oil on canvas, 72 x 60 inches
Private collection

TRANSECTION #13, 1972
Oil on canvas, 31 x 47 inches
Collection of Prudential Life Insurance Company

TRANSECTION #5, JACOB'S LADDER, 1969, Oil on canvas, 78 x 60 inches

TRANSECTION #17, 1972, Acrylic on canvas, 83 x 78 inches

TRANSECTION #19, 1972, Acrylic on canvas, 88 x 78 inches

TRANSECTION #15, 1972, Acrylic on canvas, 78 x 60 inches

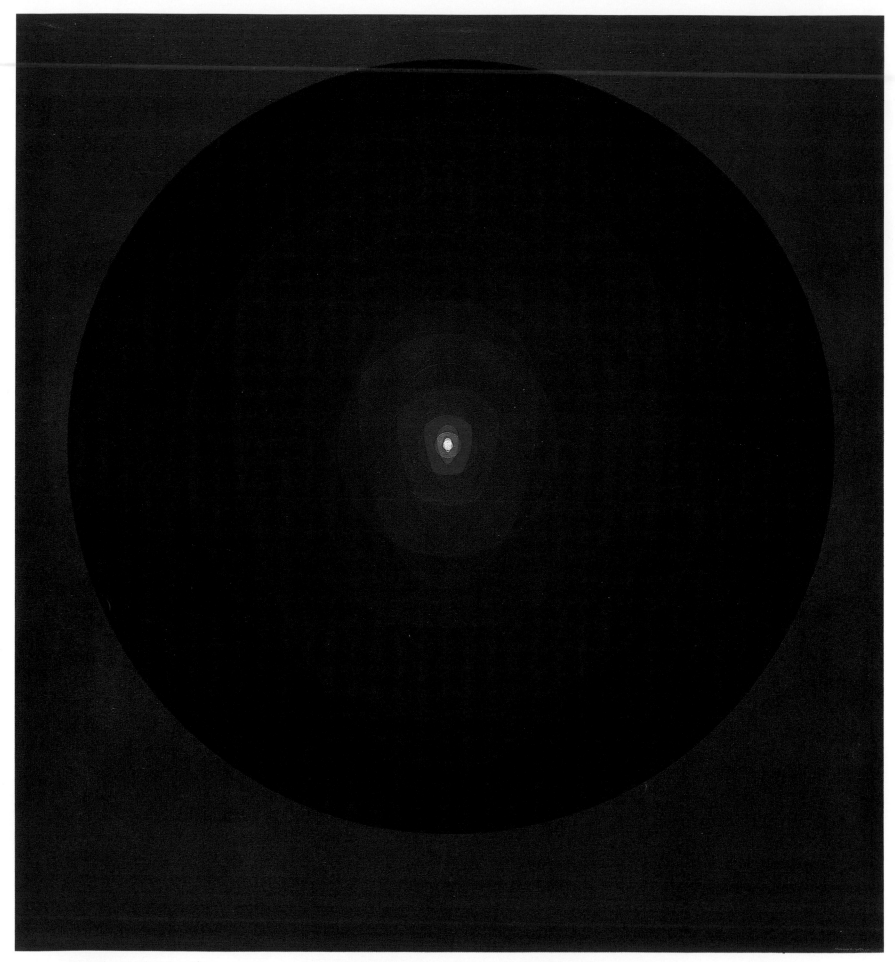

ICON-PYRRHIOUS, 1968, Acrylic on canvas, 88 x 77 inches

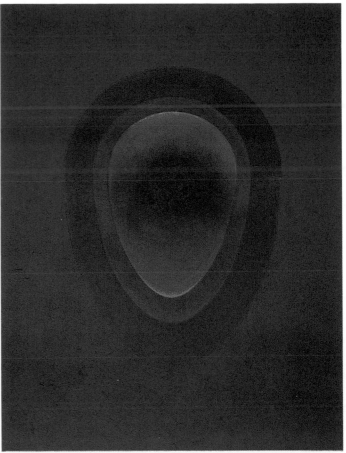

(*left*)
TRANSECTION #29, 1984
Acrylic on Scintilla
30 x 22 inches

(*right*)
TRANSECTION #30, 1985
Acrylic on Scintilla
30 x 22 inches

(*left*)
TRANSECTION #25, 1975
Acrylic on Scintilla
30 x 22 inches

(*right*)
TRANSECTION #24, 1977
Acrylic on Scintilla
30 x 22 inches

119

ESCHATOS #23, 1974
Oil on canvas, 28 x 40 inches
Collection of Helen and Michael Morris

ESCHATOS #4, 1973
Acrylic on Scintilla, 22 x 30 inches
Collection of Mr. and Mrs. Brann Wry

JOHN BUNYAN IN BEDFORD JAIL—1667, 1975
Collage, 22 x 29 inches

(opposite)
IT'S TIME, 1974
Collage, 11 x 8½ inches

126

DEPARTURE, 1981
Acrylic on canvas, 60 x 78 inches
Courtesy of Gimpel & Weitzenhoffer Ltd., New York

(*opposite*)
ASPIRATION, 1982
Acrylic on canvas, 77 x 75 inches
Collection of Ronald A. Orr

132

133
INTRIGUE, 1983
Oil on canvas, 72 x 52 inches
Courtesy of Gimpel & Weitzenhoffer Ltd.,
   New York

OSIRIS RULES, 1986
Oil on canvas, 60 x 78 inches
Courtesy of Gimpel & Weitzenhoffer Ltd., New York

134

DEPARTED, 1986
Oil on canvas, 60 x 78 inches
Courtesy of Gimpel & Weitzenhoffer Ltd., New York

TWIN TOWERS, 1987
Acrylic and pencil on Scintilla, 30 x 22 inches
Collection of Helen and Michael Morris

(opposite)

WORLDS BEYOND, 1985
Oil on canvas, 78 x 60 inches

1964
Lafayette College, Easton, Pennsylavania
Sharadin Art Gallery, Kutztown State College, Kutztown, Pennsylvania
1965
Rose Fried Gallery, New York
Gallery 10, Newsweek, New York
Lafayette College, Easton, Pennsylvania
Mickelson Gallery, Washington, D.C.
Schumacher Gallery, Capital University, Columbus, Ohio
1967
Ferry Gallery, Centenary College for Women, Hackettstown, New Jersey
1969
Cleveland Institute of Art, Cleveland, Ohio
Lafayette College, Easton, Pennsylvania
1970
University of Iowa Museum of Art, Iowa City
Lafayette College, Easton, Pennsylvania
1971
Gimpel & Weitzenhoffer, Ltd., New York
1972
Gimpel & Weitzenhoffer, Ltd., New York
1974
Bodley Gallery, New York
Fairweather Hardin Gallery, Chicago
Gimpel & Weitzenhoffer, Ltd., New York
New Jersey State Museum, Trenton
Schumacher Gallery, Capital University, Columbus, Ohio
1975
Brunnier Gallery Museum, Iowa State University, Ames, Iowa
Philbrook Art Center, Tulsa, Oklahoma
1976
Carus Gallery, New York
Gimpel & Weitzenhoffer, Ltd., New York, in association with The Twenty-Four Collection, Miami
Philbrook Art Center, Tulsa, Oklahoma
1978
Gimpel & Weitzenhoffer, Ltd., New York
Muhlenberg College Center for the Arts, Allentown, Pennsylvania
1979
Gimpel & Weitzenhoffer, Ltd., New York
1980
Hirschl & Adler Galleries, New York
Hunterdon Art Center, Clinton, New Jersey
Lafayette College, Easton, Pennsylvania
1981
Hirschl & Adler Galleries, New York
1982
Gimpel & Weitzenhoffer, Ltd., New York
1983
Kenneth C. Beck Center for the Cultural Arts, Lakewood, Ohio
Harmon-Meek Gallery, Naples, Florida
1984
Gimpel & Weitzenhoffer, Ltd., New York
Lafayette College, Easton, Pennsylvania
Newark Public Library, Newark, New Jersey

1986
Sid Deutsch Gallery, New York
Gimpel & Weitzenhoffer, Ltd., New York
1987
New Jersey State Museum, Trenton
1988
Gimpel & Weitzenhoffer, Ltd., New York
Harmon-Meek Gallery, Naples, Florida
Lehigh University Art Galleries, Bethlehem, Pennsylvania
Payne Gallery, Moravian College, Bethlehem, Pennsylvania
1989
Hirschl & Adler Galleries, New York

GROUP EXHIBITIONS

1929
"American Paintings and Sculpture Annual." Art Institute of Chicago. Carter also exhibited in the Annuals of 1935, 1938, 1941, 1942, 1943, 1944, 1946, and 1948.
"International Exhibition of Watercolors." Art Institute of Chicago. Carter also exhibited in the International Exhibitions of 1934, 1939, and 1943.
"Watercolor Paintings by American and European Artists." The Brooklyn Museum, New York
"Annual International Exhibition of Paintings, Museum of Art, Carnegie Institute, Pittsburgh, Pennsylvania. Carter also exhibited in the Annual in 1938 and 1939.
"National Watercolor Exhibition." Cincinnati Art Museum, Cincinnati, Ohio
"Annual Exhibition of Contemporary American Oil Painting." The Cleveland Museum of Art, Cleveland, Ohio. Carter also exhibited in the Annual in 1930, 1931, 1932, 1934, 1935, and 1946.
"Cleveland Artists and Craftsmen Annuals." The Cleveland Museum of Art. Carter also exhibited in the Annual in 1930, 1931, 1932, 1933, 1934, 1935, 1936, 1937, 1938, and 1939.
"Watercolors by Cleveland Artists." Memorial Art Gallery, University of Rochester, Rochester, New York
"Cleveland Artists." Milwaukee Art Institute, Milwaukee, Wisconsin
"Annual (Exhibition)." Pennsylvania Academy of the Fine Arts, Philadelphia. Carter also exhibited at the Annaul in 1931, 1932, 1934, 1935, 1936, 1940, 1941, 1942, 1943, 1944, and 1946.
1930
"Annual Watercolor Exhibition." The Cleveland Museum of Art
"Biennial Exhibition of American Oil Paintings." Corcoran Gallery of Art, Washington, D.C. Carter also exhibited in the Biennial in 1935, 1937, 1939, 1941, 1943, 1945, and 1947.
"Cleveland School of American Painters." Art Gallery of Toronto, Toronto, Canada
1931
"Paintings from the Museum's Permanent Collection." The Cleveland Museum of Art
"International Print Exhibition." The Cleveland Museum of Art
"Thirty Paintings by Cleveland Artists." Los Angeles County Museum of Art, Los Angeles, California

"Paintings by Contemporary American Artists." Memorial Art Gallery, University of Rochester, Rochester, New York
"American Scenes and Subjects." Frank K. M. Rehn Gallery, New York
1932
"International Exhibition of Etchings and Engravings." Art Institute of Chicago
1933
"American Color Prints." The Brooklyn Museum New York
"Biennial International Watercolor Exhibition." The Brooklyn Museum, New York. Carter also exhibited in the International Watercolor Exhibitions of 1937, 1941, 1943, and 1945.
"Paintings by Cleveland Artists." Museum of Art, Carnegie Institute, Pittsburgh
"Annual International Exhibition of Watercolors." The Cleveland Museum of Art
"Cartoons and Caricatures." The Cleveland Museum of Art
"Annual Watercolor Exhibition." Columbus Gallery of Fine Arts, Columbus, Ohio
"Oil Paintings by Cleveland Artists." Memorial Art Gallery, University of Rochester, Rochester, New York
"Paintings and Sculpture from Sixteen American Cities." The Museum of Modern Art, New York
"Forty-Third Annual Exhibition of Paintings." Nebraska Art Association, Morrill Hall, University of Nebraska.
"American Painting During the Past Fifty Years." Nelson Gallery, Atkins Museum, Kansas City, Missouri
"Annual Exhibition of Paintings." Sheldon Memorial Art Gallery, University of Nebraska, Lincoln. Carter also exhibited in the Annual of 1938.
"Annual (Exhibition)." Whitney Museum of American Art, New York. Carter also exhibited in the Annual in 1934, 1936, 1937, 1938, 1939, 1940, 1941, 1942, 1943, 1945, 1946, and 1956.
1934
"International Exhibition of Contemporary Prints for a Century of Progress." Art Institute of Chicago
"National Exhibition, Public Works of Art Project." Corcoran Gallery of Art, Washington, D.C.
"Drawings and Watercolors by Americans." Keppel Gallery, New York
1935
"Contemporary American Painting." California Palace of the Legion of Honor, San Francisco. Carter also exhibited at the Palace in 1945.
"American Still Life and Flower Paintings." Dallas Museum of Fine Arts, Dallas, Texas
Exhibited at Ohio State Fair, Columbus.
"Annual (Exhibition)." Toledo Museum of Art, Toledo, Ohio. Carter also exhibited in the Annual in 1936, 1938, 1940, and 1946.
1936
"International Exhibition of Etchings and Engravings." Art Institute of Chicago
"Gallery Artists." Ferargil Galleries, New York. Carter Also exhibited in "Gallery Artists" in 1939.
1937
"New Year Shows." Butler Institute of American Art, Youngstown, Ohio. Carter also exhibited in the New Year Shows in 1939, 1940, 1942, 1943, 1944, 1945, and 1946.

"National Exhibition of American Art." American Fine Arts Society Galleries, New York

"American Painting from 1860 Until Today." The Cleveland Museum of Art

"Fourteen Former Students." Cleveland Institute of Art

"Art of the Americas." Dallas Museum of Fine Arts

"Exhibition of Watercolors." New Jersey State Museum, Trenton

"Paintings and Prints by Cleveland Artists." Whitney Museum of American Art, New York

1938

"Contemporary Watercolors." Ferargil Galleries, New York

"Fifty American Prints." Ferargil Galleries, New York

"American Watercolor Exhibition." Kenyon College, Gambier, Ohio

"Paintings by Ohio Artists." Macbeth Gallery, New York

"Contemporary American Painting Annual." University Gallery, University of Minnesota, Minneapolis

"American Art Today." New York World's Fair, New York

"Thirty-Two Watercolors by Leading American Artists." University of North Carolina, Chapel Hill

"American Watercolors." Toledo Museum of Art, Toledo, Ohio

"Biennial Exhibition of Contemporary American Paintings." Virginia Museum of Fine Arts, Richmond. Carter also exhibited in the Biennial in 1942, 1944, and 1946

1939

"Annual Oil Exhibition." Ferargil Galleries, New York

1940

"Associated Artists of Pittsburgh Annual." Museum of Art, Carnegie Institute, Pittsburgh. Carter also exhibited in the Annual in 1941, 1942, 1943, and 1944.

"National Competitive Exhibition." Grand Rapids Art Museum, Grand Rapids, Michigan

"National Art Week." The Metropolitan Museum of Art, New York

"Annual Exhibition." Nebraska Art Association, Morrill Hall, University of Nebraska

"Semi-Centennial Annual Exhibition of Oil and Watercolors." Nebraska Art Association, Morrill Hall, University of Nebraska

1941

"Survey of American Painting." Museum of Art, Carnegie Institute, Pittsburgh

"Fifty Great American Painters." Ferargil Galleries, New York

"Paintings from Late 17th Century to Present." The Metropolitan Museum of Art, New York)

"Watercolor Painting in the United States." Worcester Art Museum, Worcester, Massachusetts

1944

Exhibited at the Chautauqua Art Gallery, Chautauqua, New York

"Paintings by American Artists." Detroit Institute of Arts, Detroit, Michigan

"Annual Exhibition." Los Angeles County Museum of Art, Los Angeles

"Contemporary American Painting and Sculpture." The Metropolitan Museum of Art, New York

"Artists for Victory." The Metropolitan Museum of Art, New York

"Fourth Annual Exhibition—Oils and Watercolors." Parkersburg Art Center, Parkersburg, West Virginia

1943

"Group Exhibition of Paintings by Fourteen American Artists." Detroit Institute of Arts

"American Paintings." Ferargil Galleries, New York

"American Realists and Magic Realists." The Museum of Modern Art, New York

1944

"Painting in the United States." Museum of Art, Carnegie Institute, Pittsburgh. Carter also exhibited in "Painting in the United States" in 1945, 1946, and 1953

"Portrait of America." The Metropolitan Museum of Art, New York

1945

"A Survey of American Painting from Colonial to Modern Times." Akron Art Institute, Akron, Ohio

"Group Show." Ferergil Galleries, New York

"Contemporary American Paintings Annual." Herron Museum of Art, Indianapolis, Indiana. Carter also exhibited in the Annual in 1946.

"American Watercolors." Montclair Art Museum, Montclair, New Jersey

"Special Invitational Exhibition." Philadelphia Art Alliance, Philadelphia, Pennsylvania

1946

"Two Hundred Years of American Painting." The Tate Gallery, London, England

1947

"Paintings to Live With." Montclair Art Museum, Montclair, New Jersey

"Annual (Exhibition)." National Academy, New York. Carter also exhibited in the Annual in 1948, 1949, 1952, 1955, 1956, 1958, 1959, and 1960.

1948

"Contemporary American Painting." University of Illinois, Urbana-Champaign

1949

"Pittsburgh, 1790–1949." Museum of Art, Carnegie Institute, Pittsburgh

1951

"Fiftieth Anniversary Exhibition." Toledo Museum of Art, Toledo, Ohio

1952

"Man at Work." The Denver Art Museum, Denver, Colorado

"American Water Colors, Drawings, and Prints." The Metropolitan Museum of Art, New York

"New Jersey Artists." The Newark Museum, Newark, New Jersey. Carter also exhibited in "New Jersey Artists" in 1955 and 1968

1953

"Annual Mid-Year Exhibition." Butler Institute of American Art, Youngstown, Ohio. Carter also exhibited in the Annual Mid-Year Exhibition in 1955 and 1959

"Modern Art from the U.S." Kunsthaus, Zurich, Switzerland

1954

"Twenty-Fifth Anniversary Exhibition." The Museum of Modern Art, New York

1955

"Modern Art from the U.S." Museo de Arte Moderna, Barcelona, Spain

"Five Artists." National Academy, New York

1956

"Warehouse Exhibition." The Museum of Modern Art, New York

"Special Exhibition of Prints and Watercolors." National Academy, New York

"Fifty Paintings by Living American Artists of New Jersey." New Jersey State Museum, Trenton

1959

"Ninety-Second Annual Exhibition." American Watercolor Society, National Academy Galleries, New York

"American Watercolor Society Annual." National Academy, New York. Carter also exhibited in the Annual in 1960 and 1963

1963

"American Scene Between the Wars." The Museum of Modern Art, New York

1964

"The American Scene Between the Wars." Lafayette College, Easton, Pennsylvania

1965

"The Box Show." Byron Gallery, New York

"White on White." De Cordova and Dana Museum and Park, Lincoln, Massachusetts

"Radius 5." Lafayette College, Easton, Pennsylvania

Group show. Henri Art Gallery, Washington, D.C.

1966

"Michener Foundation Collection." Allentown Art Museum, Allentown, Pennsylvania

"Federal Art Patronage, 1933–43." University of Maryland Art Gallery, College Park

"Selected Works by Contemporary New Jersey Artists." The Newark Museum, Newark, New Jersey

1967

"Pageant of Ohio Painters." Butler Institute of American Art, Youngstown, Ohio

Group show. Henri Art Gallery, Washington, D.C.

1968

"Dada, Surrealism, and Their Heritage." Art Institute of Chicago and Los Angeles County Museum of Art

"The H. Marc Moyens Collection." Corcoran Galley of Art, Washington, D.C.

"The Dominant Woman." Finch College Museum of Art, New York

"Icon-Idea." Lafayette College, Easton, Pennsylvania

"Black/White." Lafayette College, Easton, Pennsylvania

"Art from New Jersey Annual." New Jersey State Museum, Trenton. Carter also exhibited in the Annual in 1970.

"Geometric Art: An Exhibition of Paintings and Construction by Fourteen Contemporary New Jersey Artists." New Jersey State Museum, Trenton

1969

"Dada, Surrealism, and Their Heritage." The Museum of Modern Art, New York

1971

"College Faculty Exhibition." Hunterdon Art Center, Clinton, New Jersey

1972

"The Non-Objective World, 1939–1955." Annely Juda Fine Art, London, England

"Nineteenth Annual Exhibition of Contemporary American Painting." Lehigh University, Bethlehem, Pennsylvania

"The Non-Objective World." Galerie Liatowitsch, Basel, Switzerland

"The Non-Objective World: 1939–1955." Galleria Milano, Milan, Italy

1973

"Forty Years of American Landscape Painting." Gimpel & Weitzenhoffer, Ltd., New York

1974

"Contemporary Portraits by American Painters." Lowe Art Museum, University of Miami, Coral Gables, Florida

1975

"Dream World: Romantic Realism, 1930–1955." Whitney Museum, Downtown Branch, New York

"Selections from the American Print Collection." Mills College Art Gallery, Oakland, California

1976

"This Land Is Your Land: A bicentennial Salute to the Fifty States." New Jersey State Museum, Trenton

1977

"Spacescapes." Sid Deutsch Gallery, New York

1978

"Geometric Abstraction and Related Works." The Newark Museum, Newark, New Jersey

"Art Deco: Architecture and Artifacts." Museum of Fine Arts, Springfield, Massachusetts

1979

"The Public Patron." University of Maryland Art Gallery, College Park

1980

"The Cleveland Museum of Art Collects Cleveland Art at the Frank J. Lausche State Office Building." The Cleveland Museum of Art

"Buildings: Architecture in American Modernism." Hirschl & Adler Galleries, New York

1981

"Social Art in America 1930–1945," in Celebration of the Fiftieth Anniversary of the Galleries. ACA Galleries, New York

"Twenty Contemporary American Masters." Harmon-Meek Gallery, Naples, Florida

"Realism and Abstraction: Counterpoints in American Drawing, 1900–1940." Hirschl & Adler Galleries, New York

"Small Towns and Villages: An Exhibition of Paintings and Photographs, 1950–1982." Hunterdon Art Center, Clinton, New Jersey

American Art of the 1930s and 1940s. Mitchell Museum, Mt. Vernon, Illinois

"Southwestern Pennsylvania Painters, 1800–1945." Westmoreland County Museum of Art, Greensburg, Pennsylvania

"The Neglected Generation of American Realist Painters, 1930–1948." Wichita Art Museum, Wichita, Kansas

1982

"Collector's Choice." Princeton Gallery of Fine Art, Princeton, New Jersey

1984

"Highlights, Featuring Four Artists." Sid Deutsch Gallery, New York

"American 20th-Century Art." Sid Deutsch Gallery, New York

"Mathematics in Art, Geometry in 20th-Century Painting and Sculpture." Montclair Art Museum, Montclair, New Jersey

"American Art of the 1930s and 1940s." Princeton Gallery of Fine Art, Princeton, New Jersey

"The Dance." New Jersey State Museum, Trenton

"New Jersey's Curator's Choice." Robeson Center Gallery, Rutgers University, Newark, New Jersey

1985

"Realist Antecedents." Artist's Choice Museum, New York

"1918–1945: Between Two World Wars." Carnegie-Mellon University Art Gallery, Pittsburgh

"Young America: Children and Art." Heritage Plantation of Sandwich, Sandwich, Massachusetts

Exhibited in New York Fine Print Fair

1986

"The Animal Kingdom." Associated American Artists, New York

"American Paintings and Sculpture." Allentown Art Museum, Trexler Gallery, Allentown, Pennsylvania

"The Machine Age in America 1918–1941." The Brooklyn Museum, New York

"Fireworks, American Artists Celebrate the Eighth Art." Butler Institute of American Art, Youngstown, Ohio

Exhibited in New York Fine Print Fair

"Art on Paper." Weatherspoon Art Gallery, University of North Carolina, Greensboro, North Carolina

1987

"The Machine Age in America, 1918–1941." Museum of Art, Carnegie Institute, Pittsburgh

"The American Print, 1890–1950." The Amon Carter Museum of Western Art, Fort Worth, Texas

1988

"'Painting America': Mural Art in the New Deal Era." Midtown Galleries, in association with Janet Marquesee Fine Arts, New York

AWARDS

1927

Third Prize, Oil Painting, Portrait. Annual Exhibition, Cleveland Artists and Craftsmen, The Cleveland Museum of Art

1928

First Prize, Watercolor. Annual Exhibition, Cleveland Artists and Craftsmen, The Cleveland Museum of Art

1929

Third Prize, Oil Painting, Figure Composition. Annual Exhibition, Cleveland Artists and Craftsmen, The Cleveland Museum of Art

1930

First Prize, Oil Painting, Figure Composition; First Prize, Oil Painting, Landscape. Annual Exhibition, Cleveland Artists and Craftsmen, The Cleveland Museum of Art

1931

First Prize, Watercolor; First Prize, Oil Painting, Still Life. Annual Exhibition, Cleveland Artists and Craftsmen, The Cleveland Museum of Art

1932

First Prize, Oil Painting, Portrait. Annual Exhibition, Cleveland Artists and Craftsmen, The Cleveland Museum of Art

1933

First Prize, Oil Painting, Landscape; First Prize, Oil Painting, Figure Composition; Honorable Mention, Watercolor. Annual Exhibition, Cleveland Artists and Craftsmen, The Cleveland Museum of Art

1934

Special Award, Oil Painting, Figure Composition. Annual Exhibition, Cleveland Artists and Craftsmen, The Cleveland Museum of Art

1935

First Prize, Oil Painting, Landscape; First Prize, Oil Painting, Industrial; Second Prize, Oil Painting, Figure Composition; Honorable Mention, Watercolor. Annual Exhibition, Cleveland Artists and Craftsmen, The Cleveland Museum of Art

1936

First Prize, Oil Painting, Landscape; Third Prize, Oil Painting, Still Life; Third Prize, Watercolor. Annual Exhibition, Cleveland Artists and Craftsmen, The Cleveland Museum of Art

1937

First Popularity Prize. Annual New Year Show, Butler Institute of American Art, Youngstown, Ohio

First Prize, Oil Painting, Portrait; Second Prize, Oil Painting, Industrial. Annual Exhibition, Cleveland Artists and Craftsmen, The Cleveland Museum of Art

1938

First Prize, Oil Painting, Landscape and Miscellaneous; Second Prize, Oil Painting, Still Life; Second Prize, Watercolor. Annual Exhibition, Cleveland Artists and Craftsmen, The Cleveland Museum of Art

1939

Second Prize, Oil Painting, Still Life. Annual Exhibition, Cleveland Artists and Craftsmen, The Cleveland Museum of Art

1940

First Prize in Oils. Annual New Year Shows, Butler Institute of American Art, Youngstown, Ohio

1943

Second Prize in Oils. Annual New Year Show, Butler Institute of American Art, Youngstown, Ohio

First Popular Award. "Painting in the United States," Carnegie Institute, Pittsburgh

First Prize, Oil Painting. 33rd Annual Exhibition, Associated Artists of Pittsburgh, Carnegie Institute Galleries, Pittsburgh

1944

Second Popular Award. "Painting in the United States," Carnegie Institute, Pittsburgh

Charles J. Rosenbloom Award. 34th Annual Exhibition, Associated Artists of Pittsburgh, Carnegie Institute Galleries, Pittsburgh

1953

Honored for Artistic Excellence. Art Director's Club of New York City

1954

The Saturday Review's Annual Award for Distinguished Advertising in the Public Interest

1955

Honored for Artistic Excellence. Art Director's Club of New York City

SELECTED BIBLIOGRAPHY

Newspapers/Periodicals

Barr, Alfred H., Jr., and Dorothy Miller, eds. "American Realists and Magic Realists." *Museum of Modern Art Bulletin* (1943).

Borsick, Helen. "Art Homecoming for Clarence Carter." *The Plain Dealer,* Sunday Magazine (April 13, 1969).

Brown, Gordon. "Clarence Carter." *Arts Magazine* (June 1976).

———. "Clarence H. Carter." *Arts Voices (Summer 1965).*

———. "Two Worlds of Clarence Carter." *Arts Magazine* (November 1966).

Campbell, Lawrence. "A Tomb With a View." *Art News* (May 1971).

Carter, Clarence Holbrook. "Advocates Constant Experimentation for Artistic Growth in Watercolor." *American Artist* (December 1958).

———. "Artist-Advertiser Relations." In *Work for Artists,* ed. Elizabeth McCausland. New York: American Artists Group.

———. "The Artists Say." *Art Voices* 4, no. 3 (Summer 1965) :3.

———. "The Devil Loves the Artist." *College Art Journal* 10, no. 4 (Summer 1951) :413–17.

———. "I Paint as I Please." *Magazine of Art* (February 1945): 46–49.

———. "Presenting Clarence H. Carter." *American Artist* (December 1945): 26.

———. "The Water Color Page." *American Artist* (December 1945): 52–53.

"Clarence Carter." *Arts Magazine* (June 1974).

"Clarence Carter: A Creative Realist." *Art News* (June/July 1943).

de Breuning, Margaret. "Carter in Review." *Art Digest* (January 14, 1944).

Dreishpoon, Douglas. "Clarence Carter." *Arts Magazine* 58 (May 1984): 10.

Geierhaas, Franz. "Clarence Carter." *Journal of the Print World,* 8, no. 4 (Fall 1985):20.

Halasz, Piri. "Trenton Museum Honoring Carter." *The New York Times* (April 21, 1974).

Henry, Donald O. "Lifelong Search for Ultimate Answers: Clarence Carter—A Phenomenon." *The Easton Express* (May 8, 1978).

Hoffman, Joyce. "Ars Gratia Artis: 6 Local Heros, Six Artists Who Do Us Proud." *New Jersey Monthly* (April 1984).

Hundley, Richard. "Clarence Carter's America." *Cleveland Magazine* (August 1975).

Information et Documents (Paris) (April 1955). (Reproduction)

Jewell, Edward Alden. "Art Shows Offer Striking Contrast." *The New York Times* (November 28, 1941).

———. "Clarence Carter." *American Artist* (November 1946).

Kent, Norman. "The Creation of a Clarence Carter Painting." *American Artist* (November 1946).

Kirkwood, Marie. "Carter's One-Man Show Melds Art and Science in Vivid Curves." *The Sun* (April 17, 1969).

Licht, Matthew. "Clarence Carter." *Arts Magazine* (October 1982).

New York Herald Tribune (November 30, 1947). (Reproduction)

Oberbeck, S. K. "The Egg and Eye." *Newsweek* (May 31, 1971).

Pau-Llosa, Ricardo. "Clarence Carter, Maestro de la Pintura del sueno." *Vanidades* (Continental) 22, no. 13 (June 23, 1982).

———. "The Dream of Order: Four Approaches to Identity and Flux in Art." *Dreamworks* 4, no. 2 (1984–85).

———. "Stairs and Ovoids: Symbols in Clarence Carter's Art." *Arts Magazine* (September 1982).

Raynor, Vivien. "A New Carter Exhibition at the Lafayette College Center." *The New York Times* (June 10, 1984).

Redd, Penelope. "Clarence Carter, Artist Here, Tells of Work." *Pittsburgh Sun-Telegraph* (November 11, 1929).

Salpeter, Harry, "Carter Prizewinner." *Esquire* (November 1945).

Schiff, David. "Carter and the Egg—The Journey Continues: Artist Probes the Essence of Life.' *The Easton Express* (April 20, 1984).

Seldis, Henry J. "La Cienaga Center." *Los Angeles Times* (October 29, 1971.)

Zimmer, William. "Clarence Carter: Enigma." *The New York Times* (December 16, 1984).

Books

American Art in The Newark Museum. Newark, N.J.: The Newark Museum, 1981, pp. 232, 307.

American Realism: Twentieth-Century Drawings and Watercolors from the Glenn C. Janss Collection. New York: Harry H. Abrahms, in association with San Francisco Museum of Modern Art, p. 209.

American Traum und Depression 1920/40. Berlin: NGKB, 1980, pp. 270ff.

Baigell, Matthew. *The American Scene: American Painting of the 1930s.* New York: Frederick A. Praeger, 1974, p. 207.

Barr, Alfred H., Jr. *Painting and Sculpture in The Museum of Modern Art.* New York: Simon & Schuster, 1948, p. 160.

Boswell, Peyton, Jr. *Modern American Painting.* New York: Dodd, Mead, & Co., 1940, p. 60.

Bruce, Edward, and Forbes Watson. *Art in Federal Buildings.* Vol. 1. *Mural Designs, 1934–1936.* Washington, D.C., 1936, pp. 45, 194, 261, 262.

Cahill, Holger. *American Art Today.* New York: Blanchard Press and National Arts Society, 1939, p. 57.

Gruskin, Alan D. *Painting in the U.S.A.* Garden City, N.Y.: Doubleday & Company, 1946, p. 153.

Hall, W. S. *Eyes on America: The United States as Seen by Her Artists.* New York and London: The Studio Publications, pp. 142, 147.

Handbook of the American and European Collections. Springfield, Mass.: Museum of Fine Arts, 1979, p. 74.

Heller, Nancy, and Julia Williams. *Painters of the American Scene.* New York: Galahad Books, 1982, pp. 68, 96, 98.

Hetzler, Florence M., and Austin H. Kutscher, eds. *Philosophical Aspects of Thanatology* (Vol. 1 of 2). MSS Information Corporation; distributed by Arno Press, 1978, pp. viii, 31–36, 101-C, 101-D.

McCurdy, Charles, ed. *Modern Art: A Pictorial Anthology.* New York: Macmillan Co., 1958, pp. 146, 181

Miller, Dorothy C., and Alfred H. Barr, Jr., eds. *American Realists and Magic Realists.* New York: The Museum of Modern Art, 1943, pp. 32, 33.

La Pintura Contemporanea Norteamericana. New York: The Museum of Modern Art, 1941, pp. 36, 114.

The Roosevelt Era. American Heritage, vol. 14. New York: Dell Publishing Co., 1963, pp. 1232–33.

Pictorial History of Catholicism. New York: Philosophical Library, 1962, jacket illustration.

Pinckney, Josephine. *Splendid in Ashes* (a novel). The Viking Press, 1958, jacket design.

Rubin, William S. *Dada, Surrealism, and Their Heritage.* New York: The Museum of Modern Art, 1968, pp. 186, 230.

Seems Like Romance to Me: Traditional Fiddle Tunes from Ohio. Gambier, Ohio: Kenyon College, in association with the Gambier Folklore Society, 1985, cover art.

Wilson, Richard Guy, Dianne H. Pilgrim, and Tashjian Dicran. *The Machine Age in America 1918–1941.* New York: Harry N. Abrams, in association with The Brooklyn Museum, 1986, pp. 255ff.

Wixom, Nancy Coe. *Cleveland Institute of Art: The First Hundred Years 1882–1982.* Cleveland, Ohio: Cleveland Institute of Art, 1983, pp. 30ff.

INDEX